The
Elementary
Principal's
Personal Coach

This book is dedicated to all hard-working school administrators and prospective school administrators. The leadership of a principal makes a difference in the lives of children and families and leaves a legacy for years to come.

The following letter was written to a particular school principal at a particular time but is dedicated to all principals. May we never forget what it is all about!

Dear Principal,

My class is writing letters to you to show how much we appreciate you, and because we know how much work you have done. We just wanted to give you a break. Anyway, you are the best principal I have had since I've been going to school. I'm not just saying that. You're the best because you help people, and you take time out of your day to help kids, maybe even teachers. Well, all I have to say is, "Keep Up the Good Work."

Taja

In Memory of Joel

The
Elementary
Principal's
Personal Coach

Tapping Into Your Power for Extraordinary Leadership

Diana Raney Williams
Essie Hayden Richardson

Foreword by Shirley M. Hord,
Scholar Laureate, National Staff Development Council

CORWIN
A SAGE Company

For information:

Corwin
A SAGE Company
2455 Teller Road
Thousand Oaks, California 91320
(800) 233-9936
Fax: (800) 417-2466
www.corwin.com

SAGE Ltd.
1 Oliver's Yard
55 City Road
London EC1Y 1SP
United Kingdom

SAGE India Pvt. Ltd.
B 1/I 1 Mohan Cooperative Industrial Area
Mathura Road, New Delhi 110 044
India

SAGE Asia-Pacific Pte. Ltd.
33 Pekin Street #02-01
Far East Square
Singapore 048763

Printed in the United States of America

Library of Congress Cataloging-in-Publication Data

Williams, Diana Raney.
The elementary principal's personal coach : tapping into your power for extraordinary leadership/Diana Raney Williams, Essie Hayden Richardson; forward by Shirley M. Hord.
    p. cm.
Includes bibliographical references and index.
ISBN 978-1-4129-8666-3 (pbk.)
    1. Elementary school principals. 2. Elementary school administration. 3. Educational leadership. I. Richardson, Essie Hayden. II. Title.

LB2831.9.W54 2010
371.12′011—dc22   2010011771

This book is printed on acid-free paper.

10 11 12 13 14 10 9 8 7 6 5 4 3 2 1

Acquisitions Editor:	Hudson Perigo
Associate Editor:	Joanna Coelho
Editorial Assistant:	Allison Scott
Production Editor:	Amy Schroller
Copy Editor:	Adam Dunham
Typesetter:	C&M Digitals (P) Ltd.
Proofreader:	Victoria Reed-Castro
Indexer:	Judy Hunt
Cover Designer:	Rose Storey

CONTENTS

FOREWORD

Coaching has become ubiquitous; it is everywhere—and for good reason. Research studies, beginning several decades ago, have informed us about the effectiveness, and thus the value, of coaching for corporate executives, for educational leaders at the district and campus level, for teachers at the classroom level, and—for an ever-increasing number of staff in the work place—across an infinite number of professions.

A MODEST LOOK AT RESEARCH ON COACHING

School-Change-Process Research

In the mid-1970s, longitudinal studies of change in schools and universities were designed and conducted by researchers at the Research & Development Center for Teacher Education, at The University of Texas, in Austin (Hall & Loucks, 1977; Hall & Rutherford, 1976; Hall, Wallace, & Dossett, 1973). The studies targeted understanding and insights that would support and assist innovation implementation in educational settings. Successful implementation was expected to lead to improvement of educational practice and, subsequently, increased successful student learning.

These studies were initiated as a result of the unsuccessful experiences of educators who introduced changes of curriculum and instructional strategies, perpetuating an annual cycle of introducing change, being provided modest support, assessing the impact of the change—typically there was little—and rejecting the effort because it was an unworthy product, and starting anew.

Along the way, some wise individual suggested that the fault lie not with the product being adopted and subjected to implementation but with the process.

Researchers at the R&D Center were invited and mandated to explore this issue.

Investigation across multiple years of study at multiple sites nationwide revealed useful findings—findings that could be employed to insure that innovations became implemented and transferred to classrooms where the change in practice might influence student results. Reports of the major findings (currently reported by Hall & Hord, 2006) included the following requirements for successful change:

1. A clear vision of the intended change (implemented in a high-quality way);

2. A plan for reaching implementation and articulation of needed resources;

3. Investment in professional learning (in order to use the "new" effectively);

4. Assessment of the progress of implementation;

5. Provision of continuous support and assistance; and

6. A context conducive to change and improvement. (Hord, Roussin, & Sommers, 2010)

The fourth and fifth strategies, assessing implementation and providing support, may easily be translated into coaching—identifying where and how help is needed by individuals and responding with needed information, skills development, or application to the work place.

Because of their importance statistically in the change process, R&D Center staff labeled these assess-and-assist strategies as "one-legged interviews," as they were of short duration and informal tone. The assessments with individuals were conducted at scheduled times, but more frequently initiated by the change facilitator while interacting with implementers on the way to the cafeteria, while collecting mail at the staff mailboxes, or crossing the parking lot to their cars at the end of the workday. Support and assistance followed, dependent upon the assessment made. Over time, the staff referred to these interactions as "little things mean a lot" after a popular dance tune of the time, because they were deemed very powerful, although they required small amounts of time and effort.

Staff-Development Research

In a similar time frame, Bruce Joyce and Beverly Showers (2002) initiated investigations into the early mysterious and generally misunderstood processes of staff development to identify the effectiveness of its phases or stages. The phases identified by Joyce and Showers are

- Study of theory;
- Modeling and demonstrations;
- Practice and low-risk feedback; and
- Peer coaching.

Like Hall and Hord (2006), change research that identified the large group-learning sessions of staff development as an important intervention to support change of practice, Joyce and Showers' (2002) studies, in addition, confirmed the importance of addressing and responding to individuals' adult learning issues in order to implement new practice in classrooms. This line of research added additional visibility to the significance and need for one-to-one or small-group follow-up with implementers, subsequent to the typical large-group learning sessions.

Joyce and Showers (2002) also found that the coaching of implementers was the most powerful factor that provided them with the knowledge, skills, and capacity to transfer the adult learning to the work place. As a result, Joyce and Showers have consistently and persistently promoted the follow-up coaching phase of professional learning as vital to implementation success.

Research on Professional Learning Communities

More recently, in the past decade and a half, the professional learning community (PLC) has become the innovation du jour, and language about it, from a wide variety of interpreters, has found its way across the nation and around the globe. Referring to the research studies conducted on PLC, a synthesis of the components, attributes, or dimensions of effective PLCs can be found in Hord and Sommers (2008). These dimensions are

- Shared beliefs, values, and vision of what the school should be;
- Supportive and shared leadership;
- Intentional collective learning and its application;
- Supportive conditions, both structural and relational; and
- Shared personal practice.

Note again that school and classroom practice is made public, in shared personal practice. In the PLC, the expectation is that administrators and teachers will invite colleagues to observe their work, script notes, and engage in a follow-up conversation that includes both "warm" and "cool" feedback. The intention is to address the knowledge and actions and behaviors of the professionals in order to support them in avoiding confusion and clarifying misunderstanding as they learn more deeply and clearly how to employ new practices so that their students achieve increased results.

Once again, while collective (large-group) learning sessions are deemed critical, the follow-up and coaching of colleagues working and watching each other while implementing the learning from the large-group sessions leverages the learning. It is an important strategy that increases the adoption and implementation of new practice.

COACHING

Who, Where, and Why

A most useful reference that provides information about the work and impact of coaching on classroom practice is that of Killion and Harrison (2006). They note the wide array of differing types of coaching for classroom personnel: challenge coaching, cognitive coaching, collegial coaching, content-focused coaching, instructional coaching, mentoring, peer consultation, peer coaching, and technical coaching (pp. 12–13), to name a few. In the corporate sector, multiple types of coaching are similarly found.

At a more descriptive level, Killion and Harrison (2006) explained the 10 roles of coaches typically found in the nation's schools. A modest adaptation of these roles has been included by Hord et al. (2010) in their volume of learning opportunities for PLCs. These roles include resource provider, data coach, curriculum specialist, instructional specialist, mentor, classroom supporter, learning facilitator, school leader, catalyst for change, and mediator (pp. 197–199). It is not difficult to imagine the breadth of knowledge and array of skills required of these coaches.

A structural demand is that of time and place for the coaching activities to be conducted. Typically, coaching is done in the teacher's classroom, thus providing an easy answer to the location issue. What is not so easy is the question of when the coaching and its subsequent follow-up consultation can be done. In too many cases, the coaches have a classroom teaching assignment in addition to coaching, making the scheduling of this activity challenging. A great deal of time, energy, and resources have been funneled into the logistics and preparation of coaching for improving teacher practice. But, what coaching for the school's administrator?

THE PRINCIPAL

Critical in How a School Operates

Since the early eighties, the research and educational literature has been replete with studies of principals—what effective principals do, how they implement their role, how they engage staff in their work for the increased learning of students, and other topics.

"Principals, specifically, are the lynchpins of school change, providing the necessary modeling and support required for a learning school" (Hord & Sommers, 2008, p. 28).

It is an established fact that principals are a most significant factor in whether the school is a learning and improving school or whether it is more likely to operate in a culture characterized as laissez faire. It is also well known that principals gain most of their knowledge and skills for "principaling" while on the job. Further, their context is one of relative isolation, as their days are filled (to a large degree) with unanticipated events that demand immediate attention; and, they most often have no administrator colleagues with whom to interact in the school. The climate across schools all too often is one of competition for principals, so that seeking colleagues for assistance or support is not politically wise. What to do?

THE PRINCIPAL'S PERSONAL COACH

With scholarly insight strengthened by reflection on the national Interstate School Leaders Licensure Consortium Standards (Council of Chief State School Officers, 1996), and, importantly, with the detail of their own experience as principals, Diana Williams and Essie Richardson fill this significant gap for the developing principal. Potential and practicing principals find a wealth of content and its application to guide their learning activities. Not only does this volume enable the learning school administrator to gain understanding of the effective principal's role but it also enables the administrator to self-assess and consider the possibilities of adopting unfamiliar practices into his or her own repertoire.

Most assuredly, a personal coach can be a significant addition to the resources provided to principals for continuing their professional learning and its application. In the current economic environment, providing this service for many schools' and districts' leaders is nearly impossible. As an effective alternative, the authors of this book provide engaging stories, rich descriptions, and serious questions that the reader can employ for growth and development. Hence, it is a valuable resource and should be found on every school administrator's worktable, dog eared and sticky noted.

For the principal, the authors are the leadership coaches, who in the text ask readers to reflect upon their own situations. The reader who agonizes over decisions is supported by the coaches who understand that many principals "cannot show their vulnerabilities" and need guidance and assistance. The authors-coaches provide a mirror and questions that stimulate readers to respond with their best thinking while "uncovering the inner resources to accomplish extraordinary results."

The book does not gloss over the challenges that principals meet daily in their schools. Indeed, Williams and Richardson draw on and share their own personal experiences as school administrators, while framing their questions and suggestions in the language of school-leadership standards. Used appropriately, this richly developed text will help principals reach improved practice that results in higher-quality teaching and subsequently increased successful student learning.

—Shirley M. Hord, PhD
Scholar Laureate
National Staff Development Council

As an elementary principal, have you ever put a child in time out then forgotten that student only to remember later when the child awakens from a nap? Have you ever accidentally put the whole school on safety alert without intending to? This book has been written to share with the reader the powerful and real stories about the elementary principalship. Some of the stories are funny, and some are sad. Some of the stories are sticky issues. Some of the stories invite reflection, and some of them invite laughter. All of them are intended to provide the reader daily insights about the realities of the principal's chair. Stories are frozen moments in time when people remember what they were doing and how they felt at the time the story was unfolding. We have learned some of our most valuable lessons about leadership from these stories. Whether you are a new administrator or a seasoned one, this book will resonate with you. You will come to find that you are not alone in your role. This book will be a good friend by your side to prevent the feeling of isolation when anomalous circumstances occur. You will come to understand that all of us, no matter how accomplished or experienced, have had similar experiences that defy logic or graduate school theory. Each day brings fresh challenges, new stories, and new lessons learned about our work.

Another educator asked me recently if there was anything that could improve schools, or were they just a lost cause. I reflected on that for a moment and then went into a litany of the factors that make a school effective. As I talked, I realized that my colleague had a glazed-over look and said, "Yes, yes, I've heard it all!" And of course, we've all heard it all. Most school leaders have been exposed to the literature that says if certain conditions are present in a school then the school will be effective for every student. A summary of some of these reform variables are included in Chapter 7. The principal's role is

critical in each reform model included. The Council of Chief States School Officers (Interstate School Leaders Licensure Consortium, 1996) have concluded a study and process where they have identified the critical standards of excellence for a principal. The Interstate School Leaders Licensure Consortium (ISLLC) standards were developed by the Council of Chief State School Officers (CCSSO) and member states. Copies may be downloaded from the Council's website at www.ccsso.org. These standards are widely accepted as the standard for principal leadership. These standards are

Standard 1: A school administrator is an educational leader who promotes the success of all students by facilitating the development, articulation, implementation, and stewardship of a vision of learning that is shared and supported by the school community.

Standard 2: A school administrator is an educational leader who promotes the success of all students by advocating, nurturing, and sustaining a school culture and instructional program conducive to student learning and staff professional growth.

Standard 3: A school administrator is an educational leader who promotes the success of all students by ensuring management of the organization, operations and resources for a safe, efficient, and effective learning environment.

Standard 4: A school administrator is an educational leader who promotes the success of all students by collaborating with families and community members, responding to diverse community interests and needs, and mobilizing community resources.

Standard 5: A school administrator is an educational leader who promotes the success of all students by acting with integrity, fairness, and in an ethical manner.

Standard 6: A school administrator is an educational leader who promotes the success of all students by understanding, responding to, and influencing the larger political, social, economic, legal, and cultural context. (pp. 10–21)

The purpose of this book is to bring these standards to life by telling stories of daily real-life situations in the lives of two elementary school principals. This book can be used both by individual principals and in professional-development settings with principals to provide the scenarios for rich conversations, to strengthen the leadership capacity for problem solving, to build relationships, and to get in touch with the essence of being a principal. As an individual, you can use this book in several ways. First, you can use your book to build your own leadership capacity as you read these stories of daily real-life situations in the lives of two elementary principals. Second, you can glean the lessons learned as reflected upon by the authors. Third, you can tap into your own power for extraordinary leadership by thinking about and responding to powerful questions that you might be asked about your own situations if you had your own personal leadership coach. You do in fact have a coach in the form of the mini-coaching sessions throughout this book. Fourth, you can journal about your own stories and issues as you think about your own challenges and successes. Fifth, you can think about how you implement professional learning in your own school related to the theme of each ISLLC standard. Each chapter ends with a professional-development idea or "snippet" that you can tuck away and use with your own staff. Finally, this book can be used as a text for professional learning in a university setting, district administrator training, or in a study group as a way to simulate real-life principal situations in a learning context. As each chapter is written related to a

particular ISLLC standard, stories can be used to illustrate real situations and conduct activities related to the various standards. Following a brief introduction to each chapter, there are four segments that accompany every story:

1. Lessons Learned

This is not a how-to book. There are numerous "how to be a principal" books. This book is organized around stories about something that happened in the day of a principal. The writer then reflects upon the lessons they learned from the episode. Names have been changed to protect the identities of those in the stories, and specific references to schools have been omitted or changed. One of the organizing principles of this book is that we have clustered the stories around the themes contained within the Interstate School Leaders Licensure Consortium Standards (ISLLC, 1998, 2007). At the beginning of each chapter, we have included a brief interpretation of the ISLLC standard related to the stories in that chapter. As we told our stories, we intentionally applied the lens of the ISLLC standards to our stories to determine how our behaviors as principals would stand up under the rigorous analysis of standards-based practice. Chapter 1 contains stories related to "Stewardship of a Vision." Chapter 2 tells stories about "Negotiating a School Culture of Advocacy. Chapter 3 addresses "Managing an Effective Organization." Chapter 4 tells stories about "Leading a Diverse Family and Community Connection." Chapter 5 tells stories about "The Ethics of Leadership." Chapter 6 contains stories about "Tuning Into the Larger Context." Chapter 7, as previously mentioned, references pertinent bodies of work about school improvement.

2. Mini Coaching

You will be asked to reflect upon your own story guided by powerful coaching questions designed to deepen the understanding of your practice as a principal. The questions have been developed by leadership coaches as "minicoaches" to help build your own capacity for reflecting upon and taking action in your own challenging situations. As leadership coaches and former principals, we coach hundreds of school principals who agonize over decisions they have made and decisions they must make. They agonize over school academics, students, staff relations, parent relations, relationships with their superiors, and countless other situations that make up the fabric of daily principal life. In addition, they often feel like they cannot show their vulnerabilities. The principalship is often a lonely job. The leadership coach provides a mirror and time for the practitioner to reflect their own best thinking about issues through the use of powerful questioning techniques, powerful listening, and providing a professional presence for the practitioner to think what they have never thought aloud and speak what they feel they cannot speak to anyone else. It becomes a gift of time for deep reflection, celebration of strengths, and problem solving with a trusted coach. Coaches are devoted solely to the success of their clients—with no hidden agendas. Every principal deserves a coach. This book seeks to provide the reader with a personal coach with the mini-coaching segments, asking powerful questions to bring out your own best thinking about your own daily scenarios. The questions are based on language consistent with the competencies put forth by The International Coach Federation (International Coaches Federation, 2009) and are intended to help the principal (1) create awareness around the situation, (2) design actions to address the situation, (3) plan and set goals, (4) monitor the progress of the actions, and (5) celebrate success. We do believe that taking the time to think and reflect while using the mini-coaching as a mirror will assist every principal in uncovering the inner resources to accomplish extraordinary results.

3. Journaling

Following the stories and lessons learned, there is a section for you to reflect and write your own related story. This form of professional development is a gift to the principal to guide self-reflection. These pages will serve as a diary and written record of your most memorable events as a principal. This is an opportunity for you to relive and celebrate both your own peak experiences and own moments of insanity. Do not simply survive: Love your work! Writing about a situation helps bring clarity to it as you tell the story. You will come to use your own wisdom to navigate these murky waters.

4. Professional-Development Snippets

At the end of each chapter, we have included a professional-development piece related to the standard that provides a job-embedded context for use with staff and/or parents. This book honors the standards for effective professional development as the activities described are job embedded and are related to the context of the setting, are driven by process standards, and hold the tenets of equity, quality teaching, and family involvement at the heart of the content. The National Staff Development Council (NSDC, 2001) has been the leader in setting standards and initiating the conversations for how this is to be achieved. The purpose is that "Every educator engages in effective professional learning every day so every student achieves" (p. 4). The standards for professional development include attention to the context of the setting, the process or the vehicles by which professional development will be delivered, and the content or substance of the professional development.

While several states have their own leadership standards for principals, the ISLLC standards seem to be the unifying body of work that sets the standard for practice. For purposes of comparison, the authors suggest that you check the URL address for the specific standards in your state.

We invite you to enter, reflect, and celebrate the creativity and love with which we all have nourished our craft as represented in the following pages.

Your authors

Extraordinary Gift

Reflective Mirror
Principal's Personal Coach
Leadership Results

ACKNOWLEDGMENTS

I wish to acknowledge my children, Allyson, Courtney, Whitney, and Ronnie, who constantly said, "Mom, you should write a book" as I entertained them with stories about being a principal in their formative years.

I wish to acknowledge my grandchildren, Briana, Corky, Gabby, Jordan, Kenyon, Kendall, Caleb, Elijah, and Jonathan, who keep my thoughts current and relevant and inspire me to want to make all schools extraordinary. I also want to acknowledge the memory of Joel, our little angel.

To my friend and companion, Tom, who never neglected talking through fine points with me, chauffeuring me around so I could think and write, and otherwise supported this project from beginning to end, I say thank you.

I want to thank Shirley Hord, my first coach, who coached me through the concept for this book and who has written an extraordinary foreword that sets the tone for our work so brilliantly.

Finally, I want to thank the many teachers, staff, parents, and students who have come alive again for me as I have fondly relived these stories.

Diana Williams

I wish to thank my husband, Walter, for his continuous encouragement and support during this whole process. He was not only my "helpmeet," but also my best critic when he challenged me for clarity of thought as he read through the material; he also brought comic relief when laughter was most appropriately needed.

I wish to thank my daughter, Karen, for her untiring efforts to supply me with reference materials and paying my overdue library fines, and my son, Kevin, who prided himself in challenging me to reach new levels in my reflections.

I wish to thank my granddaughter, Brittni, and grandson, Theodore, for who they are and who they will become as a result of the current and future educators in their lives. I thank them also for the joy and pleasure they have given to me throughout their youthful lives.

Last, but not least, I offer a great big thank you to the staff, parents, and students who gave so freely of their time, talent, and effort. Without their involvement and commitment, the school would not have been able to accomplish its mission or vision.

Essie Richardson

We wish to acknowledge and thank our editor, Hudson Perigo for her constant encouragement, belief in our ideas, and her tough love to get the job done. Also we wish to thank the many dedicated people at Corwin, especially Allyson Sharp, Allison Scott, Joanna Coelho, Amy Schroller, and Adam Dunham, who joyfully bring the process together.

We wish to acknowledge our colleagues at Coaching for Results, Inc., who continue to inspire us and set the bar high for extraordinary results in schools through coaching.

We thank the hundreds of educators, support personnel, students, and parents who keep schools going—no matter what else goes on in our society. They are the ones who provide the context for ongoing stories.

We raise our glasses to ourselves as coauthors. As we brought our own special talents together for this collaboration, we couldn't help but think that our shared experiences and friendship is a model for every principal to cultivate with another. This experience has been invaluable to both of us.

Essie and Diana

Diana Raney Williams, PhD, PCC, is a leadership coach with Coaching For Results, Inc., where she serves as Chief of Evaluation Services and as a member of the board of directors. She is a consultant with the HOPE foundation and consults across the country in professional-development activities related to school improvement, school leadership, and leadership coaching. She served as an urban educator for over 30 years in the Columbus, Ohio, City School District. In addition to being an elementary teacher and evaluation specialist, she also served as a principal, a staff-development supervisor, and a central office administrator for Effective Schools. She designed and implemented a parent- and community-involvement initiative for the district. She has authored several articles, which have been published in The Journal of Staff Development, including "Kent Elementary—A School That Can" and "Building Systemic Change Through Staff and Community Collaboration." She was a featured principal in an article entitled "Principals as Staff Developers: A Portrait of Diana Williams."

She served as a member of the board of trustees for the National Staff Development Council and is a Past President of the board. She was cofounder and Past President of the Staff Development Council of Ohio. She was awarded the prestigious Distinguished Service Award from the National Staff Development Council in 2005.

Diana served as a program coordinator and a leadership coach for Ohio State University. There, she supervised students and provided leadership coaching to accelerated administrative candidates. She also served as editor for the Ohio State University Web publication, The Principal's Office.

In addition to her work with educators across the United States, Diana has presented and consulted in China and Africa.

Essie Hayden Richardson, MEd, LPC, is a retired school administrator who currently owns a supplemental education center that provides educational services to over two hundred students in an after-school program. She also continues to provide services as a researcher for the State of Ohio through a third-party provider. Essie is a leadership coach with Coaching for Results, Inc., where she serves as a member of the evaluation team. During her career as an active educator, she enjoyed a variety of assignments that included elementary and middle school teacher, guidance counselor, staff-development specialist (founding member of the school district's original staff-development team), and elementary principal; after retirement, she continued her services to the district as a mentor principal, customer service specialist, assessment team leader, leadership coach for elementary and middle school administrators, and consultant for private schools.

She maintained throughout her career an association with various professional organizations where she served in a leadership capacity as President and board member of the Columbus Elementary Principals Association, Treasurer and board member of the Columbus Administrators Association, Urban Affairs Committee member and trainer with the Ohio Association of Elementary School Administrators, building representative and chairperson of different committees with the Columbus Education Association, National and State delegate to NEA and OEA, State Secretary for Pi Lambda Theta, and member of the Ohio Department of Education's Fairness and Sensitivity Committee that reviews all proposed test items developed for inclusion on the K–3 Ohio achievement tests.

Richardson has visited schools and interacted with school administrators in South Africa and Japan, and she has provided consulting services to missionaries in India. Her current interest is helping others to maximize their potential through coaching and training. **xix**

Dear Principal,

Thank you for making our school a better place. I fixed up a little poem about what the world would be like without you:

When the eagle forgets how to fly,

And it's 100 below in July,

When violets turn red,

And roses turn blue,

Something is missing, it's you . . .

CHAPTER

Standard One

A school administrator is an educational leader who promotes the success of all students by facilitating the development, articulation, implementation, and stewardship of a vision of learning that is shared and supported by the school community.

STEWARDSHIP OF A VISION OF LEARNING

A school is often the lengthened shadow of its principal.

—Anonymous

INTRODUCTION
Expectations + Vision = Achievement

Great schools reflect great principals. The principal is essential to the purpose of a school. In purposing, it is the principal's responsibility to develop with input from other staff members a set of core values that will move the school toward its goal of reaching high academic achievement for its students and helping a staff to become independent thinkers and problem solvers. The principal is the steward of the school. He or she drives the change that is needed to improve. Often, we think of a steward or stewardship as it relates to a labor union or religion, but it is very applicable to the principalship. In medieval times, under the feudal system, the steward or "keeper of the hall" was responsible for the management of the household; the principal has the responsibility for moving the school forward toward academic excellence. The steward needed to hold himself accountable for all that took place, even though he could delegate certain activities; in a school, the principal delegates, but maintains accountability. The medieval steward made it his business to know all the operational details of the estate; in schools, it is the principal's responsibility to have knowledge of all the details that can or might impact the mission or vision of the school. In medieval times, the steward provided the necessary training to those that he supervised and helped them to develop the skills of a good steward; in schools, the principal uses strategies that empower staff and provides training opportunities for increased effectiveness in the delivery of instruction. The principal seeks to develop stewards of education within the staff. The best principal, like the best steward, understands his or her role in the educational process and carries it out with devoted and steady effort.

The principal or educational leader must have a vision of learning. This is critical to the success of the school. Vision serves as a source of energy that drives all decisions related to the welfare and improved education of its student body and staff. It is the force that shapes the practices within the school. Without a vision, our teaching and learning activities will not contribute to significant student learning, and our efforts will be less meaningful. The vision for helping students to achieve academic excellence should be shared by all the stakeholders; it should be creative and obtainable. According to Gordon Calwelti, great leaders do just two things—they decide what to do, and then seek support to get things done (Owings, 2003, p. 47).

The principal, as the chief steward, has the responsibility of creating a learning community that will support necessary change to improve and maintain high student achievement. The teachers and staff, through professional-development activities, are invited to co-create the vision and engage in practices that reflect that vision. They also become stewards of the vision as understanding and acceptance develops, which impact practices in the classroom and eventually the readily acceptance of the established vision by the student body. When the norm of the culture changes and students begin to believe in the school, they begin to set and meet the higher expectations as established by the vision.

Beacon of Light

If we don't stand for excellence, who will? We are the keepers of the educational beacon of light!

—Diana Williams

I was so excited about my first assignment as principal. I had been assigned to a 100-year-old building in the heart of the city. The building had its own charm, with large wooden-floored hallways. There were large expanses of Plexiglas windows on the new addition and updated entranceway.

I began going in weekly during the summer as soon as I received the assignment, getting myself ready for my new role in the fall. The first time I went in, I met the custodial staff. I commented on the beautiful updated entranceway and how it would "look so nice once the windows were cleaned." I commented how I wanted to start bringing in plants to adorn the entranceway. When I went back the next week, my indirect comments had gone unheeded, so I reiterated my wishes this time a little more assertively, "Could you please clean the windows soon, so I can start bringing in the plants?" The headman, a little unkempt himself, nodded and said, "Sure, Miz Williams, we will." I went away satisfied that I had asserted my leadership and that my wishes would be carried out.

Needless to say, this game went on for a few more visits. Each time, Mr. J would be very compliant, but nothing ever changed. I thought about my response for the fourth or fifth time, and decided I was going to use my excellent persuasive communication skills this time. When we had exchanged the usual pleasantries, I said, "Mr. J, I have asked you several times now to clean the entrance windows, and you have not done so. Will you please tell me why you have not done this?" To which he replied, "Well it's like this, Miz Williams, as soon as we wash the windows, these kids are going to come up here and put their hands all over them, and then we'll just have to wash them again. It's just not worth it to wash them before we have to." My response is known to my colleagues and friends as "The Beacon of Light Speech." I stood on my soapbox with a flame in my eyes and said something like this,

> Mr. J, this school is going to be the beacon of educational light in this community. If the kids dirty the windows, we'll wash them again! This is going to be the place where everyone wants to go . . . If we don't stand for excellence, who will? We are the keepers of the educational light. We must not forget that!

After a few minutes of stunned silence (I even stunned myself), he muttered, "Well alright, Miz Williams. We'll get right on it!" Which, they did. Not only did he clean up the windows, but he also had on a new shirt the next time I came. We walked the building together, and he proudly pointed out improvements he had made for our beacon of light! We went on to have a good working relationship, and he took great pride in being the headman of the beacon of light in the community.

My Journal Story

Lessons Learned

- It is important to be direct in communication. Tell people what you want.

- Bracket your requests with specific information, such as, "I'd like this done by Wednesday of next week."

- The principal sets the tone for high expectations. Principals must convey these expectations to others and get them to buy in to them.

- People will rise to the occasion if we believe in them.

- Tell people the "whys." Telling the whys helps people understand the vision.

- Differentiate between a request and a nonnegotiable. Often, matters that are nonnegotiable are phrased as if the other person can either accept or deny the request. It is important to be clear about what we want from others.

- It is important to understand the other person's point of view.

- People will rise to higher standards if the expectation is set.

Mini Coaching

- What communication skills do you use to help others be clear about what you stand for?

- What are some strategies you have used to work with people who have disappointed you?

- What do you want for your school?

- How do you communicate your expectations to staff?

A Time for Action

The time is always right to do what is right.

—Martin Luther King, Jr.

This particular day, all seemed right with the world. There were no challenging or urgent responsibilities within my immediate awareness that needed attention; yet, I was feeling a pull at my inner being that was causing a lot of turbulence—somewhat of an anxiety attack. The cause of this condition was not clear, but as I started to reflect upon some of my earlier thoughts and observations that I gathered from the staff, I realized that change had to be initiated. Was dissatisfaction with many aspects of the school that I had responsibilities for leading causing my subconscious to drive my conscious self into action? If so, how was this transformation going to occur? How was I going to get the staff on board, a staff that had embedded itself into a belief that mediocrity in teaching performance was acceptable because of the suggestion that poverty and lack of parental involvement and concern were to blame? This was in direct conflict with how I perceived our students and their families. This difference in perceptions caused much of my emotional stress. Something had to change. On this day during my walkthrough, I decided to look for people who by their actions demonstrated a strong passion for maximizing the learning environment of their classroom.

By the end of the day, I had identified and selected 3 out of 18 classroom teachers to engage in discussing or sharing a vision of how our school could be improved academically and socially. During the individual conversations, I was pleased to discover that their beliefs were similar to mine—a belief that changing the way we as a staff did business could increase the number of successful students, decreasing the number of failing ones. The gnawing at my inner conscious seemed to decrease after each conversation. I felt more at peace because now I had started on my journey of sharing my vision and developing a plan that involved others in helping to create a more effective school culture.

My Journal Story

Lessons Learned

- It is important to develop an understanding of your subconscious.

- It is necessary to identify people who can assist you in accomplishing your vision.

- Change is difficult for some people even though it may be in the best interest of the organization.

- Established norms are difficult to change.

- As you move through your school, choose a specific point of interest to focus upon.

Mini Coaching

- Tell about a time that you have been unsettled about the direction and vision for your school.

- As you think about the changes that you want to occur, what barriers are the most daunting?

- How will you be able to move your initial intentions to deeper and more significant involvement?

The Broken Windows

We shape our buildings and thereafter they shape us.

—Winston Churchill

Like so many times before, I submitted a work order for the replacement of the glass-block windows that cascaded across the front of the building and above the library. The school district's maintenance department responded by sending a work crew to fix the problem that was caused by some of the neighborhood students who found the windows to be quite useful for target practice; they threw rocks at them during evening hours and weekends. This time, to my surprise, the maintenance men came prepared to cover the windows with wood. I was definitely not in agreement with that decision and stopped the work order by requesting they put the wooden boards back on the truck and leave the school grounds, which they did.

I immediately phoned the director of maintenance and questioned the decision that was made to cover, not replace, the windows. I was told that it was a matter of finance and that the school district could not afford to continue replacing the glass block. I explained to him that I could not afford to have the windows in the library blocked or covered with any type of opaque material. Boarded windows would take away the sunlight that streamed through the windows, thus creating a dark cavernous environment. One of our goals was to create a learning climate that was warm, inviting, and welcoming. The boarded windows would not support that goal and would expand and reinforce the negative and blighted conditions of the surrounding neighborhood. I acknowledged respectfully the district's position in this matter, but I could not and would not accept that decision. After much discussion, I was finally asked for an alternative solution. I promptly suggested the placement of a wire mesh guard over the windows to prevent the vandalism. Due to my steadfast objection, the decision was rescinded and my suggestion was followed. The installation of the wire guard protected the windows from flying objects and allowed light to filter into the library. The problem related to the broken windows was permanently solved.

My Journal Story

_____

_____

_____

_____

_____

_____

_____

_____

_____

_____

_____

_____

_____

_____

_____

_____

Lessons Learned

- When you truly believe in something and act upon your beliefs, you will be successful in your endeavor.

- The school district has to be fiscally responsible, but not at the expense of my students' welfare.

- Be prepared to fight for the interest of your students.

- I was willing to be labeled uncooperative if that had been the outcome resulting from my actions.

- Develop an understanding of your challenges and have feasible solutions to problems when asked for input.

Mini Coaching

- Tell about a problem that you want to resolve.

- How will you make your wants clear?

- How will you be clear in your thinking so that you can present your case in a clear and concise manner?

- What other possibilities can you think of to resolve your problem? Think of at least five. Now, think of five more.

Controlling the Louse

As the wound inflames the finger, so thought inflames the mind.

—Ethiopian Proverb (Leslau, 1985)

The mission statement of our school implied that it was our purpose to maximize the learning opportunity for each student. In reaching this goal, it was necessary to recognize and alleviate any condition that might interfere with this outcome. For whatever reason, our student body was plagued with head lice. I suspect it was the result of transmitting the bug from to head to head by way of the old stuffed furniture that sat on the porches of many homes in our school community, the sharing of head wear and hair implements, or the affectionate contact that primary-grade children, especially, have with each other. Whatever the reason, we had more than our share of this social problem.

Once a child became identified as having head lice, he or she, according to our board policy, was removed from school. For readmission, the student's hair needed to be cleaned by combing out the lice and nits, treated with some type of medicated shampoo, and screened by the school nurse. This was an expensive and time-consuming activity; many of the parents could not afford the shampoo, and the nurse who worked in our school on a part-time basis was not always available. Some of the parents became upset about the removal of their children and reacted by not attending to the situation as promptly as possible. The absence, although necessary, was in conflict with our mission statement of maximizing the learning opportunity for each student. This was a challenge that needed to be resolved. The staff and I had to come up with a plan that enabled our students to be in school, adhere to board policy, and protect the unaffected population. After much discussion, we created a mini health clinic, which was staffed by one of our educational assistants who was very passionate about keeping the kids in school. Our focus was to assist parents in combing out the lice and nits while at the school. We were also able to provide shampoo, donated by our local pharmacies, to the parents who needed it. Selected school staff also performed the head check when the nurse was not on duty. A very negative situation was turned into a positive one. Once parents viewed the school as having a genuine interest in helping resolve the problem and did not regard it as a stigma, parents became positive about doing their job in controlling the problem. Absence created by head lice was practically eliminated.

My Journal Story

Lessons Learned

- The incongruence between our mission statement and the practice of removing students for head lice was a concern. How can students be expected to learn when they are not in school?

- Certainly, it is the parents' responsibility to ensure that their children's education is not disrupted, but we cannot control the actions of parents.

- We as a school staff have the responsibility of engaging in practices that support our beliefs.

Mini Coaching

- From the examination of data, what solutions can you think of to address your issue?

- What can you control, and what type of actions could be taken that will resolve your issue?

- How will you involve the staff in solving this problem?

Keeping the Kids at the Center

Set the tone for a child-centered mission.

—Diana Williams

Upon entering my new assignment as principal, I noticed that staff members began jockeying for little perks, usually beginning with, "The former principals did it this way," or "The former principals allowed us to . . ." I made it clear even as we reviewed our mission statement that central to all decisions would be what's best for the children.

There was a large, spacious, carpeted room that apparently a former principal had agreed to let one of the kindergarten teachers move to. On the other hand, there were two teachers who had been researching team teaching and multiage grouping who wanted to develop a model for the school in first and second grade. This model would include up to 50 students and two teachers as opposed to the 23 students for the kindergarten room.

Other faculty members generally supported my decision that the multiage group would be better served from the room usage. While the kindergarten teacher was disappointed, I do believe that she also came to view this as a wise decision, as it was made based on the question "What's best for the most children?"

My Journal Story

_____

_____

_____

_____

_____

_____

_____

_____

_____

_____

_____

_____

_____

_____

_____

_____

Lessons Learned

- Adhering to the vision allows for better decision making and buy in from a broader base.

- Modeling the importance of keeping students at the core of the vision sets the tone for a child-centered mission.

- You cannot always please everyone when making a decision.

Mini Coaching

- When have you had to make a decision that disappointed a staff member?

- How have you been able to foster collaborative decision making?

- How have you used your mission statement to drive a decision on behalf of students?

The Unstoppable Event

The secret of success: Never let down! Never let up!

—T. Harry Thompson

The Boy Scouts of America in our area were concerned about the lack of availability of scouting opportunities in communities that experienced a lower socioeconomic status and, therefore, created a program that would bring scouting to the central parts of the city through the in-school Scouting program. Our school was identified as a potential prospect for the program. After much discussion, the teachers and I felt that it would bring a different set of opportunities to our students and we accepted the Scouts' offer to implement the program in our building. Learning modules that embraced the academic standards of our district as well as the Scouting curriculum and experience were designed. Our in-school Scout leader was extremely dedicated to her work with our students and worked diligently to help our fifth-grade students develop the necessary skills to participate in a citywide first aid competition. It was very exciting to have our team excel at the district, state, and finally the national level. Since our school had many challenges, both social and academic, this level of success was a morale booster for the student body as well as the immediate community.

One of the rewards for coming in first place nationally was the opportunity to be recognized during the annual conference of the American Red Cross. We received a congratulatory letter that also invited us to the conference. We became really excited about having our students engage in this type of experience; but one week later, our excitement ended when a representative from the Red Cross contacted me. She attempted to discourage the team from attending the national event and indicated that our plaque would be mailed to the school. Of course, I would not accept the suggestion. Realistically, it was going to be a stretch of the imagination to transport our students to Baltimore, Maryland. Money was the biggest issue along with time and travel arrangements. I was determined that our students would have their recognition; they worked hard to earn it, and this was a rare opportunity for them to travel beyond their community. With donated money, I was able to buy airline tickets and arrange limousine service from the airport to the conference hotel. Several of the parents came with us. Neither the students nor the parents had flown, so this trip provided exceptional opportunities for the group. The trip was a one-day event; we left at 6:25 a.m. and returned at 6:35 p.m. This was one of my most rewarding accomplishments—just to be able to help provide this experience to our families and to participate and share the joy of our time together.

My Journal Story

_____

_____

_____

_____

_____

_____

_____

_____

_____

_____

_____

_____

_____

_____

_____

_____

_____

Lessons Learned

- As the building principal, it is my responsibility to take advantage of the opportunities to have my students experience activities beyond their daily lives.

- I have the ability to create within each student the desire to strive continuously for success and to understand the rewards and recognitions that come from hard work.

- In your walk as an administrator, it's difficult to know when and how you affect the lives of your students unless you are fortunate enough to receive a note years later from one of them who indicates a desire to be just like you (what an honor).

Mini Coaching

- Think of a meaningful accomplishment you have made on behalf of students.

- In what ways did the outcome outweigh the time and energy required to accomplish this goal?

- What indicators would you use to determine the benefits of the experience?

- How did you obtain the resources needed for your goal?

Field Trip to a Great School

Professional learning together builds a strong learning community that improves outcomes for students.

—Diana Williams

In our district, there was one school in particular that was making a name for itself by implementing a comprehensive and effective schools model. The principal was a well-known and highly respected leader. The school had been promoting its mission as an outstanding academy for poor and minority children. They had implemented several innovative curricular approaches, they had opened up a parent center on their premises, and they were fostering high expectations among their student body by promoting an academic and safe climate. In short, as a principal taking on a failing school, I wanted us to do, have, and be all that the other school promised.

This Academy hosted visitors on certain days of the week at particular times as their reputation grew. I engaged enough substitute teachers over the course of a month to allow each staff member to spend a morning at one of the sponsored tours at the Academy. I asked that they take note of those things that the other school had and were doing that would be good for our school. Also, I asked them to note things that we were doing as well or perhaps better than the other school. I asked them to hold their comments and notes until everyone

had a chance to go. Finally, all of the staff had visited the model school. The secretary, custodian, and I were the last three to go.

The following week, we had a staff meeting where we put up chart paper labeled with the characteristics of effective schools:

- Strong leadership
- Climate conducive to learning
- Monitoring of student achievement
- High expectations for everyone
- A strong parent and community focus

We then listed in columns all of the ideas that we saw that we would like to implement. We also used a column to list some of the things that were occurring at our school that we were proud of and wished to retain. Once all of the ideas were on newsprint, everyone had three sticky dots to use to vote and prioritize their most pressing areas of concern. From that process, we engaged committees willing to work in the prioritized areas. Ultimately, these areas would become our school-improvement plan, which became the guiding document for our reform work and our grant writing.

My Journal Story

_____

_____

_____

_____

_____

_____

_____

_____

_____

_____

_____

_____

_____

_____

_____

_____

_____

_____

Lessons Learned

- The field trip, as a form of professional development, helped to jump start our thinking about how we could be a truly great school.

- We were able to recognize some of the growth we had accomplished as well.

- This process facilitated the staff coming together as a team to accomplish our goals.

- This reaffirmed my belief that professional learning—together—builds a strong learning community that improves outcomes for students.

Mini Coaching

- How do you foster learning opportunities for your staff?

- How do you assure follow-up and implementation of the professional learning?

- How do you align professional learning with outcomes for students?

- How is the professional learning embedded in best practices at the school?

The Winds of Change

Things do not change; we change.

—Henry David Thoreau

Our school district, like most public schools, uses data to determine the impact of its educational programs on the various populations that are served. As our school was a Title I school, we had access to grant money earmarked for school improvement. I have always believed that if you keep doing the same things in the same way, you will end up with the same results. It was necessary to infuse the minds of the staff with fresh ideas regarding teaching and learning if real change was going to occur, which meant that we would need to go beyond the walls of our school. In consultation with the Title I district administrators, a school on the East Coast was selected for a site visit. I shared the opportunity with the staff and explained why it was necessary for us to visit an exemplary school that had socioeconomic conditions similar to ours but a higher rate of success in their efforts to overcome them. It was also important to acknowledge that our students performed well, considering the perceived history that each child brought to school, but it was possible to improve that performance if we changed our teaching methods, organization, expectations, and classroom-management styles. The opportunity to explore and the challenge to become better at what we do were presented to the staff. The staff bought into the idea of visiting another school to obtain information that would act as a catalyst for our desired change. Four teachers, divided evenly between primary and intermediate levels, were selected for the experience.

The day before we departed for our site visit, I made sure each team member was prepared with the necessary information regarding flight numbers and time, name and address of the school, knowledge regarding ground transportation, and the need to arrive at the airport in a timely manner. Upon my arrival at the airport, a few minutes behind schedule, I encountered a rather long line, which delayed my getting to the gate prior to the closing of the jet way. I missed the plane. However, I was able to catch the next available flight and joined my team about an hour after their arrival at the school, amid their good-natured teasing as well as their relief from the uncertainty imposed by my delay. All went well after that incident as we began to focus on the school and its program. We observed the utilization of all staff in the delivery of the reading program and the enthusiasm that seemed to radiate throughout the entire school. We saw teachers using effective techniques of instruction and classroom management, and students actively engaged in the learning process. We were provided the opportunity to discuss the school's program with teaching and support staff and to do some videotaping of the school. It was a very impressive experience.

The visit was successful and it accomplished what it had been designed to do. It had a profound impact on the team and created the energy that was needed for them to influence the other staff members. The team provided the leadership that encouraged the teachers and support staff to want to take a serious look at what our students needed and how those needs could be met. It was amazing to witness the effect of exposure to a positive teaching-learning climate; our team bubbled with the possibilities of what could happen in our school. It enabled our staff to reflect more objectively on their abilities to make a difference in the lives of our students and for change to become a reality rather than a passing thought.

My Journal Story

_____

_____

_____

_____

_____

_____

_____

_____

_____

_____

_____

_____

_____

_____

_____

_____

_____

Lessons Learned

- The desire to change must be kindled similarly to starting a fire.
- Change occurs best when others become involved in the process.
- Make sure you heed the advice you give to others.
- Knowledge, when used for the right purpose, provides the fuel for action.

Mini Coaching

- What indicators for success do you have for your school?
- What opportunities have your staff members had to expand their vision of success?
- What opportunities for collaboration are you thinking of?
- How will you know when you have achieved your goal?

Holding High Expectations for Report Cards

Before we can demand excellence from students, we must first demand it of ourselves.

—Diana Williams

Prior to sending out the first set of report cards in my first year as principal, I asked the teachers to prepare their report cards, including all notes they were sending, and send them to my office for review. I communicated to them that I wanted (1) to become acquainted with the student records and to identify students who might be having academic difficulty, (2) to become acquainted with the grading patterns of the teachers, and (3) to proof the letters and notes that went out from our school. We had had initial talks about "academic excellence" and the vision that each child was going to be successful. I was surprised to find numerous spelling errors, grammatical errors, rub-outs, strike-outs, and write-overs in the notes provided by a number of the teachers. While I thought I would be making a cursory inspection of the report cards and taking notes on student progress, I ended up gathering a large pile of sticky notes and flagging many mistakes. I asked those with extensive errors to redo the report cards and resubmit them to me

before sending them out. It was a lot of work for me to pore over almost 300 reports, but the alternative would have been to convey to our community that we accepted low performance on the part of the staff. How could we be a beacon of excellence when we had low expectations for ourselves? Through the course of massaging some hurt feelings and holding the vision for excellence before them, we got through the first round of report cards. I also encouraged them all to proof any correspondence going out from the principal's office to make sure there were no mistakes. From that moment on, everyone took pride in the materials that were sent out. On the next round of report cards, some teachers attached sticky notes to their cards saying that they had checked them over and hoped there were no mistakes. On other occasions, some would impishly and with great delight point out errors in some correspondence I might be sending out. I took it with grace and pride that we were all embracing the same vision of excellence.

My Journal Story

Lessons Learned

- People want to do a good job.
- Telling people the "Whys" of your requests helps them to either buy in to a common vision or reject it. More often, they will buy in.
- Leaders must hold themselves to the same standards that they hold for others. A leader must "walk the talk."
- Before we can demand excellence from students, we must first demand it of ourselves.

Mini Coaching

- Think of a time that you were productive in an excellent setting. What were the attributes of that setting that promoted excellence?
- What are the attributes of the vision that you seek for your school?
- How are you able to hold excellence up as a desirable attribute for your staff?
- What strategies have you used to promote excellence within your staff?
- How will you know that your staff embraces a vision of excellence?

Professional-Development Snippet

Vision Requires Change

Change has a considerable psychological impact on the human mind. To the fearful it is threatening because it means that things may get worse. To the hopeful it is encouraging because things may get better. To the confident it is inspiring because the challenge exists to make things better.

—Whitney King, Jr.

Change denotes making or becoming distinctly different and implies either a radical transmutation of character or replacement with something else. Applied to our school, change was the process of transforming our current organizational practices into new behaviors that supported a shared vision of learning. Kurt Lewin's (2006) force field analysis was selected as the initial tool to help us to move in the direction that was needed for our success. We chose a process that would help us to identify significant factors that could impact our school's ability to change. Lewin's tool allowed the school staff to identify the issues that impeded or supported the creation of a learning environment—a place that sustained the academic, social, and personal growth of all our students. In the world of schooling, we have all types of people—those who make things happen, those who watch things happen, those who ask what happened, and those who actively seek to keep things from happening. It is difficult getting rid of those imbedded cultural practices that fail to nurture the academic success of all students, albeit the results of such practices are not intentional. An example of a practice that might be considered favorable is the creation of a system to reward students for good behavior by having a weekly extra recess that places one teacher on duty while the others attend to "teacher business." In this or similar situations, the question becomes who is benefiting from the reward. If the teachers are concerned about what the students are learning or how much more the students should be

learning, time is an asset, and we need to take a closer look at how it is used. A disconnect, in situations such as those illustrated by the example referring to the use of time, existed between that which was expressed and which was practiced.

The challenge of sharing the vision was how to give all the "stakeholders" in the organization an opportunity to express their opinions in a safe and supportive environment. The force field analysis process provided each staff member the opportunity to be involved in identifying issues related to continuous school improvement, the driving forces that encouraged change and the restraining forces that maintained the status quo. The instrument used to create a visual of the generated information was a simple diagram created by drawing two columns on large sheets of newsprint and heading the left column as Driving Forces and the right column as Restraining Forces. After the issues to be discussed had been prioritized, a single issue was placed on top of the T-shaped diagram. The influencing factors were identified, placed in the appropriate column, and positioned to illustrate their strengths or organizational influence; strong forces were placed farther away from the middle of the equilibrium line, and weaker forces were placed closer to the middle line. Arrows that extended from each written factor were drawn pointing toward the center. As a result of identifying change issues and factors that supported or hindered progress, it became apparent what could be changed, how it could be changed, who could provide the necessary influence to make it happen, and how the change could be sustained. This process of staff development is not the single dose of vaccine that provides a lifetime remedy; it is a series of doses that must be continued frequently after

initiation and revisited over time. Figure 1.1 describes the continuous process of visioning, sharing the vision, planning and designing actions, evaluating results, celebrating successes, then starting the process over again.

Figure 1.1 Cycle-of-Vision Process

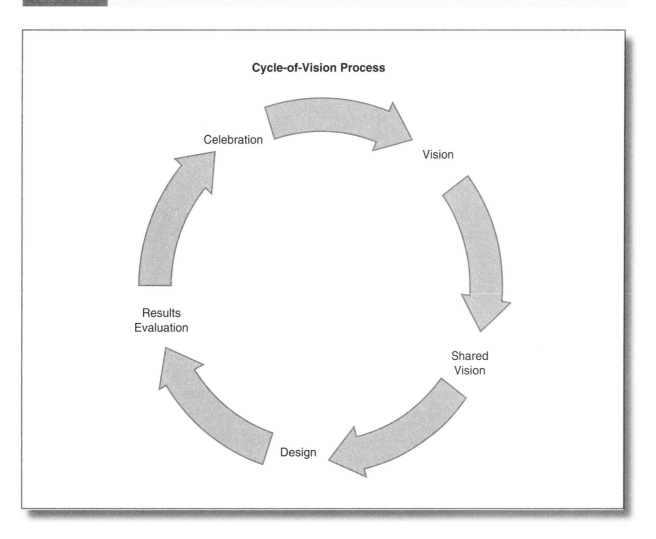

In reality "learning" and "change" are synonymous. Change is not an issue if it makes sense to and is "owned" by those involved, rather than being arbitrarily imposed. An appreciation that change is a continual process, involving confusion and difficulty, is vital for future learners. "It is not change that kills, it is the transitions."

—Anonymous

OUR SCHOOL'S CYCLE-OF-VISION PROCESS

Kurt Lewin (1951) theorized that there are three stages to change:

1. Unfreezing

   An organization has to rid itself of old practices and ideas before it can adapt new behaviors. This is not easy because habits are hard to break.

2. Changing

   This phase of the process involves a mixture of confusion and excitement due to the uncertainty of the new as well as its promise. A good deal of patience and cheerleading is required for the successful transition from the old to the new to occur.

3. Refreezing

   Once the changes are in place and the new behaviors are apparent through what is observed within the organization, it is important to celebrate the successes and begin the process of preparing for the next change process.

Based upon Lewin's work, the staff entered into the first stage of change by attempting to unfreeze many of the old practices that failed to help the staff and students achieve the results that were desired. The services of the school district's staff-development office were used to facilitate the staff-development activities. Substitute teachers were obtained, and we were able to provide release time for staff to meet during the school day. In addition to full day inservices, after-school staff meetings, as designated in the teacher's union contract, were used for staff-development activities related to issues that had been identified in the initial force field analysis activities. Routine information that sometimes can become the focus of regular staff meetings was handled through written communication, thus recognizing and honoring the staff's ability to read and understand, as well as making more efficient use of time. School people are appreciative of small acts of kindness, so refreshments were always a part of those activities that required the sincere efforts on the part of the participants. As one administrator, a friend of mine, once said, "A staff runs on its stomach."

Dear Principal,

I hope you have a great Christmas holiday. You worked hard. You make a great Principal. Christmas is special and you are special too. Enjoy the Christmas holidays.

Your friend,

Shanae

Dear Principal,

You have worked hard and you need a break. You have helped the school very much to get through problems. If you weren't here, I don't know where we'd be. I will maybe go to my sister's on Christmas. Maybe you should go home and spend Christmas with your family. Nice talking to you.

Aaron

CHAPTER

Standard Two

A school administrator is a leader who promotes the success of all students by advocating, nurturing, and sustaining a school culture and instructional program conducive to student learning and staff professional growth.

NEGOTIATING A SCHOOL CULTURE OF ADVOCACY FOR STUDENTS

To lead people, walk beside them . . . As for the best leaders, the people do not notice their existence. The next best, the people honor and praise. The next, the people fear; and the next, the people hate . . . When the best leader's work is done the people say, "We did it ourselves!"

—Lao Tsu

INTRODUCTION
Staff Learning = Student Learning

The stories in the following pages show the heart and soul of schooling embodied in this standard. There are two parts to this standard: (1) the instructional program that fosters a culture conducive to student learning and (2) leading the learning environment through staff professional growth. Much has been written about both. These stories are examples of creating a collaborative culture that supports student learning, leadership that creates structures for strong professional learning, and using data to drive the learning and leading.

LEADING THE INSTRUCTIONAL PROGRAM THAT FOSTERS A CULTURE CONDUCIVE TO STUDENT LEARNING

A high-performance culture is one in which everyone is a leader, and everyone is a learner, to assure a quality instructional program conducive to student learning. All stakeholders within the culture listen and speak to each other in ways that foster deeper understanding, mutual respect, and positive energy. In this type of culture, there is a common language that says, "I care about you," and, "I can count on you." Even under a cloud of personal or organizational challenge, individuals can rely on each other. The school often functions as a family unit with all of the corresponding interpersonal dynamics. The goal is for everyone to feel like they belong and that there is a climate of trust and support.

Significant change in organizations begins with significant changes in what leaders think (conceptual clarity in both the depth of their understanding and their beliefs), what they say (their degree of courage), and what they do (their commitment). Leaders can have impact on the professional learning of the staff even in incidental hallway conversations with individuals throughout the day. Leaders can transmit their views by listening and having genuine dialogue.

That's what leadership in professional development is all about—helping people be better. In the movie, *As Good as It Gets* (Brooks, Zisken, & Andrus, 1997), Jack Nicholson's character says to Helen Hunt's character, "You make me want to be a better man." There is the power to be a better person within us all. Just like when Dorothy, the Scarecrow, the Tin Man, and the Cowardly Lion, in *The Wizard of Oz* (Fleming, Leroy, & Freed, 1939), went to the Great OZ to get something, they found they had what they needed within themselves all along. Leaders that inspire us to be our best selves hold and act on the belief that we can all grow and get better.

What a Collaborative Culture Isn't

It isn't coming up with a good idea yourself and then getting the staff and faculty to go along with it.

It isn't making all the plans then asking them to rubber-stamp the plans.

It isn't giving them what they want.

It isn't saying, "I did . . ."

It isn't filling a staff meeting with "administrivia" announcements and pronouncements.

What a Collaborative Culture Is

It is searching the hearts and minds of your teachers for their ideas and feelings on a particular topic.

It is allowing them to try and possibly fail at an experiment that they have truly thought out and planned. If they are successful, it is celebrating their pride in their accomplishment. If they are not successful, it is celebrating the learning that occurs as a result of their failure.

It is understanding that your vote counts, too. As the leader, you can be clear about your veto power when the situation dictates that a decision is non-negotiable. Being equally clear that if a situation does not demand a nonnegotiable solution, you will have a vote in the say just like everyone else, with majority deciding. Be clear about the ground rules.

It is collaborating that mediates and facilitates the thinking of the group. Proceedings are clearly communicated to all stakeholders.

It is taking out the *I* and inserting *we*.

It is co-creating staff-learning and meeting opportunities for dialogue and problem solving.

A collaborative culture embodies a leadership model that focuses on building the capacity in others to share accountability and ownership rather than one leader assuming all of the responsibility for the situation. A collaborative culture requires asking and listening rather than directing and telling. A collaborative culture is open and transparent rather than tightly controlled and non-sharing. Leaders in a collaborative culture are dynamic and seek to build the capacity both within the organization and within those with whom they work.

Traditional hierarchical-leadership practices called for leaders to tell their staff what to do and how to do it. The leader was the expert with all of the answers. New leadership practices embrace the idea that there are multiple stakeholders with great expertise. When all ideas are considered and nurtured within a collaborative culture, there are far greater results for the organization.

As coaches, we have seen examples of various leadership styles. The more-collaborative leadership styles are congruent with the competencies outlined by The International Coach Federation. We refer to this leadership behavior as "coachlike behavior."

Reilly and Williams (2008) have provided a conceptual way to view leadership practices as "coachlike" behaviors, as seen in Table 2.1.

The effective leader operates from the coaching zone. As leaders move from the supervisory zone to the coaching zone, there is greater collaboration, as relationships are co-created through effective communication, listening, and collaboration. Staff members can more readily come together to create, design, plan, monitor, and celebrate together.

LEADING THE LEARNING ENVIRONMENT THROUGH STAFF LEARNING

Negotiating a school culture of advocacy for students requires an attention to the skills of the staff. Attending to the skills of the staff requires resources to support adult learning and collaboration. The heart and soul of professional development is the context, the content, and the processes used to get results (National Staff Development Council, 2001). The context of the adult learning is embedded in the day-to-day work of the staff. The context requires a skillful school leader that facilitates

Table 2.1	Leadership Practices Continuum

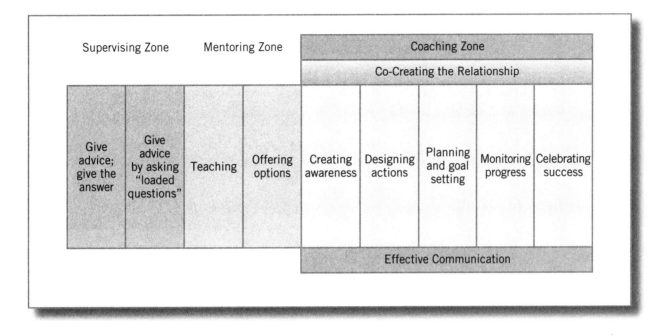

Supervising Zone		Mentoring Zone		Coaching Zone					
				Co-Creating the Relationship					
Give advice; give the answer	Give advice by asking "loaded questions"	Teaching	Offering options	Creating awareness	Designing actions	Planning and goal setting	Monitoring progress	Celebrating success
				Effective Communication					

continuous improvement for everyone through growth and learning that occurs as a routine part of the workday. The content of professional development is driven by the data that suggest what is needed by staff. The process requires multiple sources of information to guide the improvement and demonstrate the impact, including perceptual data, demographic data, student-learning data, and programmatic data (Bernhardt, 2002, p. 47). Perceptual data takes into account the perceptions that all stakeholders have of effective schooling practices. It is important to ask stakeholders what is working, what is not working, and why. By listening to students, parents, and staff, the school culture can better be understood and modified.

It's important to know your school community. Demographic data will give you a paper-and-pencil bird's-eye view of your school. There is nothing that helps you gain a greater appreciation for your community than to go into the community through home visits, neighborhood sweeps, and drive throughs. It was so gratifying to drive through the community in my big, old, blue suburban, waving to parents and kids and hearing kids shout out, "There's the principal!"

The student-learning data will provide a roadmap to having a school culture conducive to student learning. How else will you know your deficits and your strengths? Looking at disaggregated standardized assessments, teacher-made assessments, district-aligned benchmarks, attendance data, discipline data, and whatever other baseline information that you have will form the basis of planning to make your school conducive to student learning. The identified deficits will give your professional learning community the content with which to work, but the strengths will give your professional learning community the context.

It is wise that all stakeholders have clarity about your programs and processes. Keeping accurate program data is also useful when you must submit reports or write grants for resources. It is important to document what works, what does not work, and why.

A *good* leader inspires staff to have confidence in the leader. A *great* leader inspires staff to have confidence in themselves. The following stories exemplify standards-based leadership that fosters a school culture and learning climate of high expectations for students, staff, and all stakeholders. The power of leadership resides in us all.

Joey

I've come to the frightening conclusion that I am the decisive element in the classroom. It is my daily mood that makes the weather. As a teacher I possess a tremendous power to make a child's life miserable or joyous. I can be a tool of torture or an instrument of inspiration. I can humiliate or humor, hurt or heal. In all situations it is my response that decides whether a crisis will be escalated or deescalated and a child humanized or dehumanized.

—Haim Ginott, Psychotherapist and Author

This is Joey's Story. The power of our office to influence the lives of our students is awesome. We are called upon to be creative and bold in reaching out to some of our more troubled students. I had an elementary student in my building who was every principal's nightmare. He was always in trouble. He was unmotivated to do any schoolwork. He was one of the 5% Caucasians in a 95% African American school, yet he audaciously and frequently used racial insults, bringing on the wrath of fellow classmates. He was in special education, so he had certain stipulations in his IEP related to techniques and disciplines. Subsequently, we learned that he was a foster child, was depressed, and had been on numerous antidepressants at his tender age. Even later, we learned that he had mistakenly attended an "adoption party" with his three siblings. The siblings had been selected for adoption, but he had not.

On a day much like any other, Joey found himself in my office, sitting at my conference table for a time out from his classroom. I pretty much was going about my own work. At one point, he said, "Hey, Dr. Williams, your plant is gonna die." I said, "Oh, do you think so?" He said, "Yup, but I can fix it." I said, "Oh, you can?" He said, "Yup, it needs some water." I said, "Well would you like to take care of that for me?" He said, "Yup."

He got a pitcher and went to get water. He came back, and I marveled at how he fussed over the plant. He asked if he could come back the next day to check on it. The light bulb went off in my head, and I saw a golden opportunity. I said, "If you finish your work and your teacher gives you permission, that would be great."

Of course, I saw his teacher later that day and we worked out a plan that coming to care for my plant would be his reward for meeting certain goals she would set daily. The next day, he appeared at my door before lunch. He very lovingly attended to my plant. He said that it needed no more water, but asked if I'd like him to look at the secretary's plant. The secretary got in on it and agreed that her plants needed some attention, too. Soon, he was checking on the plants in the hallway. Our plants flourished, as did he. He went from being a "nightmare" to being a wonderful citizen. He managed to make friends and was chosen as a "good citizen" by the end of the year.

The story doesn't end there. He came to school before we opened in August with a woman. He explained that he would no longer be going to our school because he had been adopted over the summer and he would be moving to another school district. He said he wanted us to meet his new mother.

When I reflect upon my work, I know that Joey is what we are all about as principals. I hold this celebratory story close to my heart. It provides fuel when things get harried. I offer this as a celebration of our work and the lives we influence.

My Journal Story

Lessons Learned

- There are no "throw away" children. It is important to maintain a safe and supportive learning environment for all students, no matter how difficult.

- It is important that the staff employ a variety of techniques and creative ideas in working with all children, especially difficult children.

- It is important to apply theories of growth and development.

- Collaboration with all staff members involved with the student, parents, social-agency personnel, and special-education personnel form a team to create a safe learning environment for all children.

- It is important to find the right key to unlock the brilliance within each child, no matter how difficult they may appear.

- Never give up on an "unlovable" child. You never know when, under the right circumstances, he or she will find their wings and become loveable again!

- It is good to celebrate success and build on those successes.

Mini Coaching

- Think about your most challenging student, and ask yourself what you want for this student. Be specific.

- Brainstorm multiple ways of helping this student. Be prepared to think out of the box.

- What other persons or resources do you need to help you with this student?

- What can you do for yourself to alleviate the stress of dealing with this student?

Williams, D. (2008). "Joey" originally appeared in the *Principals Office,* an ezine for school administrators from The Ohio State University's P–12 Project and Interprofessional Commission. The *Principal's Office* is available at www.principalsoffice.osu.edu.

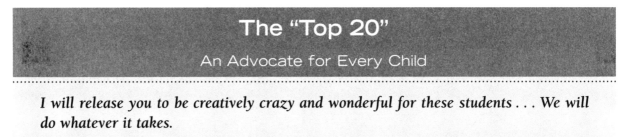

The "Top 20"

An Advocate for Every Child

I will release you to be creatively crazy and wonderful for these students . . . We will do whatever it takes.

—Lorraine Monro, Author

About the middle of the school year, certain students were beginning to present themselves as students who could use a little extra TLC. The staff got together and decided that we would collectively develop an advocacy program for students who either, by their academic performance or behavioral performance, could benefit by having extra positive attention from someone they could respond to. We developed a list of about 25 names out of a school of 385 elementary students, solicited volunteers from all staff members, and developed an information sheet on each identified student based on discipline data, report-card data, and anecdotal information. Staff members were intentional in selecting students that perhaps they had had positive interactions with outside of the classroom. Or, perhaps they had them in an earlier year when the child had experienced more success. We made the list of students and their "advocates" available to the staff. Any time a student in question ran into difficulty in the school, did poorly on tests, or otherwise needed a friendly adult to talk to, they were given the option of going to see their advocate in the school. Usually, just a few minutes of precious time from a caring adult determined if a situation would be escalated or deescalated. The caring adult made a difference in the climate for that child for that moment.

My Journal Story

_____

_____

_____

_____

_____

_____

_____

_____

_____

_____

_____

_____

_____

_____

_____

_____

_____

_____

_____

_____

Lessons Learned

- It takes a whole village to educate a child.

- Interventions for students are powerful when there is collaborative team effort on the part of the staff.

- Data must guide interventions. Continual updating of the data will show progress made with individual students.

- Follow-up support for the staff by counselors, social workers, and other professionals should be available for the adults in an advocacy program.

Mini Coaching

- How do you celebrate the successes you and your staff have had with students?

- What barriers prevent staff persons from going beyond their normal teaching assignments? What are your thoughts as you have listened to their concerns?

- In what ways do you inspire staff members to want to go beyond their usual routines to help children?

- In what other ways do you model contributing to the lives of students beyond your normal responsibilities?

Williams, D. (2008). "Top 20: An Advocate for Every Child" originally appeared in the *Principals Office*, an ezine for school administrators from The Ohio State University's P–12 Project and Interprofessional Commission. The *Principal's Office* is available at www.principalsoffice.osu.edu.

Who Will Take the Discipline Transfer?

Modeling professionalism and trust elicits professionalism and trust.

—Diana Williams

Our school had a reputation for doing a good job with students with discipline problems. We would frequently take transfers of difficult children from other schools. Perhaps it had more to do with the principal having a soft spot for difficult children. We had a process in our district for how to move difficult children to other sites. The practice was that a principal would simply call another principal and beg the receiving principal to take a difficult child off of his or her hands. If both principals agreed, the district office would facilitate the move.

With one particular student, "Anthony," the sending principal poured his heart out about all of the grief he had been through with this particular second grader and thought that if he just had a fresh start, he might be successful. I listened intently and took detailed notes. I said to the sending principal, "give me time to discuss this with my team, and I will get back to you." He was dubious with the enjoinder, "If you leave it up to the 'team,' they won't take him." Nevertheless, I agreed to get back to him the next day.

I scheduled a meeting with my second-grade team for the next morning before school. As we sat at the conference table, I explained the circumstances to them and asked them for their opinion about what we could do for this child. They acknowledged that he sounded like other children we had worked with successfully. Then, they discussed the possibilities for taking him. They looked at each of their own class compositions, the number of challenging students they already had, how the new student might potentially interact with their current students, what special programs and resources we had, and other professional issues pertaining to this child. It was much like a team of doctors deciding on a course of action to save the life of a patient. We very much felt like we were in the business of saving young lives. Finally, the team decided which classroom the new

student would best fit into. The other team members offered their support in terms of serving as "time out" for other students if needed and by being extra attentive to the new student. I asked the receiving teacher what other support she would need from me. She asked that he not start to school the next day, which was Friday, but that he start on Monday to give her time to get his "welcome badge," books, and materials together. She requested furniture for him. I agreed. We all left the meeting on one accord as if we were all a part of a great mission. The receiving teacher was revved up for the professional challenge. I called my principal colleague and informed him that our team had decided to receive Anthony. I asked that he tell the parent not to bring the child to school until Monday, and we would be happy to welcome him then.

When Monday came and Anthony reported to the office alone, from the school bus, a little dubious, with a little chip on his shoulder, I greeted him warmly and assured him that his teacher and classmates were looking forward to meeting him. Rather than dumping him in the breakfast room, I had someone bring him his juice and breakfast and allowed him to eat in a room off of the office until the bell rang. Then, I escorted him to his new room. I introduced him to his teacher who met him at the door, saying, "Welcome to our classroom, Anthony. We are so happy you are here." She introduced him to the class and took him to his new desk, where his books and supplies were neatly placed. He had a shiny nametag on his desk like the other children. The classroom "ambassadors" came to help him get settled and to show him around the classroom.

I checked with the teacher later and looked in on him. He was indistinguishable from the other children. He ultimately fit in very well, and I knew that the collaborative preparation made a difference for this "difficult" student.

My Journal Story

_____

_____

_____

_____

_____

_____

_____

_____

_____

_____

_____

_____

_____

_____

_____

_____

_____

_____

_____

Lessons Learned

- Good teachers want to do the right thing by students.
- Modeling professionalism and trust elicits professionalism and trust.
- Two or more heads in making a decision are always better than one.
- Where one culture can be toxic for a student, he or she can blossom in another.
- We are all entitled to at least one fresh start. Sometimes a fresh start makes a big difference for a child.

Mini Coaching

- What are your thoughts on teacher empowerment?
- If you say you believe in teacher empowerment, in what ways have you sought to empower teachers?
- Examine your belief system about leadership. How far will you go to empower teachers? How much do you believe in their right and ability to share the power?
- What are the benefits in teachers taking a more-active role in shared leadership?

Under Siege Before I Got Started

Co-creating thoughtful problem-solving processes overcomes defensiveness, anger, and resistance.

—Diana Williams

When I was assigned to my new school, I was told that there was a grievance pending. Grievances were formal complaints lodged by the union on behalf of teachers for alleged violations of the employee contract. I was told that the union would not withdraw the grievance despite the fact that there was a new principal until the issue was resolved to the satisfaction of all parties. The nature of the grievance was that the teachers had not approved of the duty schedule that the former principal had devised for playground and lunchroom coverage.

When I became aware of the situation, I invited any of the staff members who had a good idea for duty coverage to convene in my office on an appointed day. About five vocal teachers showed up to discuss the problem. After listening to their concerns, I asked each one of them to devise a duty schedule to bring back to the group for discussion.

I told them that I, too, would devise one, giving it my best shot. A week later, we all came together again and each person or group (they had grouped themselves) gave a short presentation of their ideas for the duty schedule. It is interesting to note that in all cases presented, the terms actually gave more duty coverage to teachers than the original plan proposed by the former principal. We looked them over and voted on one that a group of the teachers had worked on. This is the plan we all agreed upon, and we went forth to present it to the rest of the staff. The teacher group who had devised the plan presented the plan to the staff and advocated for the plan. Everyone voted, and the plan was adopted. The new duty schedule went into effect, and everyone supported it. A few days later, I got official notification that the grievance had been withdrawn.

My Journal Story

_____

_____

_____

_____

_____

_____

_____

_____

_____

_____

_____

_____

_____

_____

_____

_____

_____

_____

Lessons Learned

- Responsibility and accountability for some decisions can be shared with better results than if one person makes the decision.

- The administration and the teaching staff can be collaborators, rather than adversaries.

- Teachers are professionals; and when the expectation is that we want to do what is best for students, they will rise to the occasion.

- Co-creating thoughtful problem-solving processes overcomes defensiveness, anger, and resistance.

Mini Coaching

- Think about a time when you had a sticky staff problem. Think about the attributes of your leadership that successfully resolved the issue.

- How do you handle resistance from staff? Think of multiple ways to handle resistance.

- How do you overcome emotions in an adversarial climate?

We Will Be a Team!

The key is to replace a belief in "experts" who "deliver" knowledge of what good teaching is to workshops with communities of teachers who learn through ongoing collaboration and practice.

—Dennis Sparks,
National Staff Development Council

At one point, there seemed to be a lot of bickering and complaining about who was working harder, whose students were or were not the better behaved, which floor had more privileges, and so on among cliques on the staff. During one of our planning meetings with incessant finger pointing and complaining, I practically stamped my feet and said, "If nothing else, *we will be a team!*" That was the turning point in establishing a professional learning community. We formed a professional-development committee and began looking for opportunities to learn together and build our team. A significant number of staff attended a local conference about professional learning communities. The speaker spoke on the importance of professional learning, the importance of collaborative planning, and the importance of coming together as a team to tackle the difficult problems in schools. Staff members who sat on either side of me jabbed me during the presentation and whispered, "That's what you've been saying!" After the conference, we returned to school, and various staff members presented what they had learned. The next step was to take a significant number of staff members to a school team conference in Kansas City sponsored by The National Staff Development council. Several of us went with the caveat that everyone would share his or her session information with the rest of the staff at our annual retreat. When I asked each one how much time they would need to present what they had learned at the session, most of them said about 5 to 10 minutes. Without exception, at the retreat, each one ended up giving powerful presentations lasting much longer than 5 to 10 minutes. This necessitated readjusting the retreat agenda. The staff both enjoyed presenting and hearing from their colleagues. There was such a spirit of support and common purpose as we learned together. That was the point at which several "wait and see" and "can't be bothered" staff members got on board, and we became a team!

My Journal Story

_____

_____

_____

_____

_____

_____

_____

_____

_____

_____

_____

_____

_____

_____

_____

_____

_____

_____

_____

_____

Lessons Learned

- I relearned how powerful job embedded professional development delivered by those closest to the work can be.

- I learned to trust the professionalism of the staff. When challenged with the opportunity to deliver professional presentations, they exceeded expectations and grew not only as a team but also as individuals.

- Through this process, I came to believe in the notion of forming a professional learning community as the way to improve teaching and learning performance, as professionals learn to learn together, trust each other, and help each other.

Mini Coaching

- How do you, as the leader, find and broker excellent professional-development resources to help both yourself and your staff to grow professionally?

- In what ways are you able to build the capacity in others?

Williams, D. (2008). "We Will Be a Team" originally appeared in the *Principals Office,* an ezine for school administrators from The Ohio State University's P–12 Project and Interprofessional Commission. The *Principal's Office* is available at www.principalsoffice.osu.edu.

Math Achievers

Student engagement in high-energy academic activities fosters good discipline.

—Diana Williams

In the quest for continually high standards and success on high-stakes testing, often the simple yet obvious skill of math computation is neglected in favor of the higher-order math problem-solving skills. Our staff collectively came up with a fun way to emphasize math computation skills while not detracting from the teaching of the math curriculum as required. The "Math Achievers" program became a highly coveted recognition process among students and parents alike. It was simple. The teachers made multiple copies of age-appropriate math-computation sheets and we announced that every Friday the whole school would engage in timed math tests right after lunch. At the end of the day, students who had accomplished the 100% criteria we had established—as determined by their teachers—would be called down to the main hallway by intercom to sign their name in colorful marker on the Math Achievers Wall of Fame. The math and literacy teachers and I would shake each child's hand, and they would have to tell us which math objective they had mastered. We kept records of every students'

progress. They would receive a pencil and a treat, and their name would be published in the school newspaper. The art teacher designed a large, heavy, four-segment cardboard wall for the kids to sign on. This became a highlight of every Friday. Needless to say, the students worked extremely hard to master their math facts. Often, students would stop me in the hall during the week and say, "I only missed math achievers by one point!" The teachers who were more reluctant to do this were pressured by their students to participate, so we had 100% school participation. Parents watched for their child's name in the newspaper. I heard from one or two of them if their child's name was inadvertently left out. The math and literacy teachers and I had to keep careful records. While the math wall started out with minimal signers, it eventually filled up, as most children in the school were able to proudly point to their names. This process was very effective not only in helping children get excited about their learning but it also set a standard for academic excellence in the school for teachers and parents as well.

My Journal Story

_____

_____

_____

_____

_____

_____

_____

_____

_____

_____

_____

_____

_____

_____

_____

_____

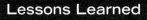

Lessons Learned

- Collaboration among staff members can take a kernel of an idea and turn it into a schoolwide project.
- Naysayers will join in if they perceive that there is some value in the activity. Excited students and parents can win them over.
- Schoolwide high academic expectations are more easily cultivated when everyone is engaged in a schoolwide project.
- Student engagement in high-energy academic activities fosters good discipline.
- It is important to think of multiple and creative ways to recognize student achievement.

Mini Coaching

- How do you celebrate academic achievement in your school?
- What ideas do you have for bringing naysayers on board with a good idea?
- What does a school that fosters high expectations for academic achievement look like? What actions or activities will you see?
- What ideas do you have to increase the academic expectations in your school?

The Spelling-Bee Craze

Enthusiasm begets enthusiasm.

—Henry Wadsworth Longfellow

The school district sponsors an annual spelling-bee contest, and our school had not participated in this activity. The two Title I reading teachers and I, after much discussion, decided to change that paradigm by at least showing up at the district's initiative. The probability of winning the contest seemed somewhat remote. At this time, our school was not recognized for its academic successes; we were clearly not the worst performing school, but definitely not the best. Our goal was to create the possibility of winning with the expectation that we would be successful. The Title I teachers developed the plans for identifying our school's representative. Each classroom participated at the beginning of the competition by holding classroom spelling contests; and through this process of elimination, the finalists were identified for the school championship round and the determination of which student would represent the school in the district's spelling bee. The upper grades, third through fifth, were invited to watch the competition, which they did in an almost "spelling-binding gaze." After what seemed like a long afternoon, the winner was declared, and preparation for the district's spelling bee started the next day.

The teachers and student gave up part of the lunch hour to prepare for the contest. The big day arrived, and we were off to the spelling-bee site. The teachers, parents, and I grew more nervous as the rounds started to fade and our student was still standing. At last, the final round ended. We won! The feeling of joy and pride could only be matched by the feelings that occur when a school wins a state-sponsored contest such as sports, music, or some other big event. The outcome of the contest had a more far-reaching effect than "we won the district spelling bee." It gave life to something that I had not identified or anticipated; it gave life or meaning to the whole school and community. After all, you share the good news by informing parents of the positive things that are happening in the building and helping them to embrace the ideals and values that are inherent in your building.

My Journal Story

_____

_____

_____

_____

_____

_____

_____

_____

_____

_____

_____

_____

_____

_____

_____

_____

_____

_____

_____

Lessons Learned

- Students will rally around a unifying academic activity, particularly if they have a sense of involvement.

- The teachers, as well as parents, were impacted by our "public" achievement; it provided them with boasting power.

- Teachers are willing to give time and energy to projects that they endorse or "own."

Mini Coaching

- What are the opportunities that you have to improve your school's image?

- What are the vehicles that might be used? What kind of image for your school would you like to achieve?

- What are the resources that you need, and who are people that will help in this endeavor?

- What gives life and meaning to your school and community?

Florida Bound

It is not what is poured into a student but what is planted that counts.

—Joel Hilderbrand,
Chemical Education (in Baughman, 1963)

The kindergarten teachers loved to catch me off guard with some idea that was not expected, anticipated, and perhaps somewhat irrational. Mary Ross came into my office and announced plans to take all 80 kindergarten students to Disney World, which is about 1,200 miles from our school. I listened to this elaborate plan and then asked the appropriate administrator's questions, such as, "How are you planning on traveling? What are you planning to do upon your arrival in Florida? When are you leaving for your trip, and how long will you be gone? What will the students learn as a result of this activity?" Each question was answered with a very matter-of-fact response; then, she added that it would take the entire school day and that I would assist at the airport check-in. The trip was an outgrowth of learning activities that centered on the environment, oceans, beaches, transportation, and the children's interest. She also explained how the trip was going to occur—which was on the school premises.

Two weeks later, the big day arrived and our kindergarteners embarked on their trip to Orlando, Florida. The three kindergarten classrooms clustered in the school's lower level, emptied into a large hallway that was transformed into the airport lobby, which was set up with ticket counters, security, and an airline gate to be used for boarding the plane located inside one of the classrooms. The plane replicated one that might be used for international flights; it had nine rows of seats with nine across and two sets of aisles, the pilot's cockpit, and flight attendants (parent volunteers) who helped the passengers find their seats and later served refreshments during the imaginary flight. After landing, the passengers disembarked from the plane and took a shuttle to their hotel where they checked in, went to their rooms (separate areas for boys and girls) to change into swimwear, and then gathered in the hotel lobby before ascending steps to the beach, which was outside in front of the building. The area was designed to have the characteristics of a beach that included places for games, sand, water, and picnicking; lunches were provided by our food service. Everyone had a great day.

During the following week, the teachers followed up on the experience by integrating it into appropriate content areas—language arts, science, social studies, music, and art.

My Journal Story

_____

_____

_____

_____

_____

_____

_____

_____

_____

_____

_____

_____

_____

_____

_____

_____

_____

_____

Lessons Learned

- It is amazing how teachers can use creativity to turn learning into a fun activity and provide students with experiences that most of the students in our school would never have.

- Listen completely and fully before speaking, and provide the needed support.

- Ask questions that help to expand ideas related to learning outcomes.

Mini Coaching

- When you have concerns about a planned activity, how do you convey your concerns to the other person?

- How do you balance honoring creative ideas and maintaining the standards as "non negotiable?"

- What deep questions will stimulate further thinking on the part of the planner?

The Teacher's Dilemma

The solution to a problem changes the nature of the problem.

—John Peers, Peers Law

Mrs. Clark was not happy with Mr. Harper, our head custodian. She indicated that she was not able to use the gym or multipurpose room at 2:30 p.m. because the custodian sets up the tables for breakfast at that time and leaves the building for the day. The 2:30 time worked best for her instructional day and provided the opportunity for her to fulfill the necessary time allocation for physical education. I asked her if she had explained the situation to Mr. Harper. She said that she spoke with him, and he said that he needed to prepare the multipurpose room for the breakfast program and did not have the time to set up the tables after she finished the class because it was time for him to go home. Before continuing, I must commend Mr. Harper for his professionalism; he took pride in his work and was highly effective in maintaining an attractive, sanitary, and safe facility for our students, staff, and public. He was very responsive to me whenever I asked him to do something; it was done immediately. I was now caught in the middle of an ongoing feud between two highly skilled individuals who were each determined to have it their way. So, both parties and I met to discuss the issue that was going nowhere. Each party explained their side of the story, and now it was time for me to make a decision. Of course, the decision was in favor of the teacher. I explained that the facility and its use were for the benefit of the students, and their educational activities were not to be subordinated to the personal preferences of any staff member. The issue of instructional use and custodial responsibilities was resolved, but not the interpersonal relationships. Mrs. Clark complained that Mr. Harper would not speak to her; unfortunately, he also stopped speaking to me, but he still performed his duties. After about two weeks of being given the silent treatment, I decided to confront him on his turf. I found him in the custodial office, pulled up a chair and started to have some dialogue about his behavior and its impact on me. I described his behavior and my responses, both immature. Our conversation ended on a cordial note and an agreement that our feud would end. The relationship that I had with Mr. Harper returned to normalcy, but the climate between him and the teacher continued to be chilly.

My Journal Story

_____

_____

_____

_____

_____

_____

_____

_____

_____

_____

_____

_____

_____

_____

_____

_____

_____

_____

Lessons Learned

- Decisions that involve students must always be made in their favor.

- It is easy to defend decisions that benefit children.

- Adults must resolve their own problems, and it happens more effectively when two people are willing to communicate with each other.

Mini Coaching

- Think of a time you had to mediate a situation between two people. What worked? What did not work?

- What were the points of view that drove the discussion?

- When interpersonal relationships are an issue, what would the ideal relationship look like, and how would it be achieved?

Good Morning, Ladies

Let us not be deceived.

—Bernard Baruch, Presidential Advisor

It was 10:30 a.m., and all of a sudden, one instructional assistant paraded past me as I stood monitoring the front hallway, then another, and another, and another until all seven assistants disappeared into the teachers' lounge. I continued on my walk through the building, while making a mental note of the incident. I concluded after conversation with myself that it was time to engage in some research, so I began to spend more time in the front hall, observing during the midmorning. Within a few days, I approached one of the assistants and made a friendly inquiry about why everyone went to the lounge at a certain time and discovered that this was their agreed-upon break time. The full-time support staff is entitled to a fifteen-minute break in the morning and afternoon. I had a problem, not with the break, but with the preciseness of the activity. The assistants were coming from different rooms within the building and there was no bell or other mechanism to signal a change in classroom routine. Since most of the assistants were providing direct service to identified students, I had difficulty imagining how everyone could bring closure to their lessons with such preciseness without some consequence. It seemed that this type of break schedule would cause some children to not receive the appropriate amount of instructional time, interfere with the flow of a lesson, or impact negatively on a classroom activity.

The common break schedule arranged by the instructional assistants did not appear to pose a concern for their classroom teachers—the issue was never raised in the advisory building-committee meeting, but to maintain such a pattern did not seem to be feasible without some type of cost. I had a situation that needed to be resolved, but in a manner that was nonthreatening, yet firm. I did not want to be accusatory without gathering additional information, such as checking with each of the teachers to see what break policies were established within their classrooms. None of the teachers had a policy regarding break time for their assistants. So, I devised a way to resolve the problem without saying a word. At their break time, I gathered up my mail and went to the teachers' lounge to work. The ladies were all there having a good time engaging in lots of conversation and fellowship. An amazing thing happened after I took my seat. The conversation ceased, silence blanketed the room, and one by one the ladies excused themselves and returned to their classrooms. For the next few days, I made it part of my schedule to work in the lounge during the midmorning, but no one joined me, and I was left to sit there by myself. This situation resolved itself without creating an issue; after all, they were responsible adults who had thoughtlessly engaged in an activity that was great for themselves but not in the best interest of our students. I did share my concerns with them by asking the question, "How was it possible to schedule a common meeting without having some classroom disrupted?"

My Journal Story

_____

_____

_____

_____

_____

_____

_____

_____

_____

_____

_____

_____

_____

_____

_____

_____

_____

_____

_____

Lessons Learned

- One must always be mindful of the practices that can creep into a school that are not in the best interest of students.

- It is important that staff members bond but not at the expense of other staff or instructional effectiveness—whether it is intentional or innocent.

- In the words of Theodore Roosevelt, "Nine-tenths of wisdom consists in being wise in time."

Mini Coaching

- Think of a time when you have wanted to confront behavior in your school that was not in the best interest of students.

- How were you able to reconcile the dilemma?

- When questionable situations arise, what do you do to resolve them?

The Meeting Is Over

If we want to help people change, it's important that we don't push or pull them—just walk together.

—Aquarian Conspiracy (www.leading-learning.co.nz)

Assuming the responsibilities of your first school at the beginning of the school year is challenging enough, but the situation can be even more insurmountable if the appointment comes after the school year starts and the previous administrator is held in high esteem by the staff. I walked into such a situation (October 24) not knowing the culture of the school and not really being accepted by the staff. As I began to become better acquainted with the staff through engaging conversations, I started to learn what my role as the administrator was expected to be. It was somewhat different than I had anticipated. One of the revered staff members was unofficially "the principal," although her real responsibility was a Title I reading teacher. She acted as the voice of the staff as well as the disciplinarian.

After being in the school for about a month, I decided to start planning for the implementation of change for the second semester. Before change could really occur, I needed to know who was influential and how the system operated. I needed to know who was willing to change and what needed to be changed. I started with what seemed to be a problem for most of the staff, which was the dismissal of the students in the evening. I must admit, things got pretty wild during that time of the day because we had an equal amount of those who lived in the neighborhood (the walkers) and those who rode the bus (the riders); there was too much crisscrossing as the students were dismissed. So, I decided that we would engage in a problem-solving staff-development activity that included everyone—professional as well as support staff; the support or noncertified staff members had not participated in previous staff meetings. To my delight, the staff came up with some brilliant suggestions on how we could improve the dismissal process. Planning takes time, and when people become really involved with problem resolution, time tends to become irrelevant. That goes for most of us, but there

is always the exception. "Miss Principal" decided that maybe things were going too well, so she stood up and declared that the staff meeting was over because we had exceeded the staff-meeting time limits as established by the union contract. I remember to this day the look on the faces of the other staff members, one of almost dismay, but because of her influence, the staff began slowly to trickle away. With the exception of a few minor details, sufficient time prior to the disruption of the meeting had enabled the staff to create a dismissal plan that would work and involved all staff. I allowed the meeting to end without challenging her, but one can only imagine the restless night I experienced trying to determine how to resolve the first obvious challenge to my leadership.

The next morning, I went to the lounge and quietly asked Miss Principal to come to my office; she complied. Once inside the office, I asked why she had dismissed the staff meeting. She responded, in an uncomfortable manner, that some of the staff had wanted her to stop the meeting; as the building representative, she was expected to intervene on behalf of the staff. At that point, I looked her in the eye and reminded her of our responsibility to the safety and welfare of our students. I continued by addressing her qualities of leadership and asking her to refocus her energy on engaging in those things that would be most helpful to the students. I was pleasantly surprised when she asked what she could do and, before I could respond, volunteered to unload our buses each morning and load them in the afternoon. The word came back to me that she returned to the lounge and told everyone how I had gotten on her case. The reasons behind the rumor I failed to understand, but it worked to my advantage and as promised, she monitored the buses every day until she retired at the end of the school year. She also wrote the nicest note thanking me for allowing her to do the job she was hired to do.

My Journal Story

_____

_____

_____

_____

_____

_____

_____

_____

_____

_____

_____

_____

_____

_____

_____

_____

_____

_____

Lessons Learned

- Sometimes, things are not what they seem to be if one takes the time and has the courage to pursue the truth.

- Silence is sometimes golden. I can only think of a teacher in the classroom who deals with an unruly student in a manner that is perceived by the other students as unfair and how, emotionally, they move toward supporting the unruly student. This can and does happen with teachers when they begin to perceive the principal as unjust and unfair.

Mini Coaching

- What do you want for your school? How can you accomplish the changes you want?

- Think of a difficult conversation you want to have with someone. Plan what you will say, and practice your talking points prior to the conversation.

- What else can you do to correct an unfortunate situation?

Empowering the Staff

Power can be taken, but not given. The process of taking is empowerment itself.

—Gloria Steinem, U.S. Feminist

The staff was poised for change. The opportunities for exploration of other schools faced with similar social and economical conditions had yielded positive results. It was discovered that our situation was not unique, and we as a staff could make a difference in the lives of our students. We stopped blaming or identifying parent apathy or the neighborhood as the culprits responsible for the lack of student achievement, and we started to view the situation from our side of the educational equation. Many of the schools that we visited were located in similar and even more impoverished neighborhoods than ours, but the students in those schools were achieving academically more than some of their more privileged peers. Our staff always took pride in its perceived ability to teach; the awareness that someone could be accomplishing more than we did or could was challenge enough to encourage consideration for change.

We collected a wealth of information and knowledge that would be used to frame our desired organization. Each staff member had the opportunity to participate in an activity that would help to broaden his or her perspectives on educational change and how our school could be transformed to meet the needs of our students. Some of the staff visited schools that were identified as models that might be considered for emulating; others attended conferences and seminars. As we worked toward common goals, a team spirit emerged that had not existed prior to the staff's commitment to change. After months of sharing, comparing, and eliminating, the big day arrived for deciding what organizational model would be used the following school year. It was decided that we would create a learning laboratory to support the work of the classroom teachers. Often, activities and plans are not going as smoothly as appearance would indicate, which occurred when one of the teachers who was not in favor of change attempted to sabotage the work of the staff by openly challenging the final plan. However, the move was quickly squashed when another staff member, one of the leaders for change, responded to the dissenter and the vote was taken to accept the plan as presented.

My Journal Story

_____

_____

_____

_____

_____

_____

_____

_____

_____

_____

_____

_____

_____

_____

_____

_____

_____

Lessons Learned

- Exposure of all members of the school community to current practices and research is essential for creating a climate for change.

- It's important to acknowledge and encourage leadership from within the staff.

- Common goals help to encourage, support, and maintain a sense of unity.

Mini Coaching

- What outcome do you want and anticipate as the staff expands its knowledge?

- As a learning community, how will you revisit your vision and mission?

- How will you know that the vision and mission is driving change?

- What would be the indicators of success?

Soar With the Eagles

It is not enough to have an outstanding professional-development program. Attention must be paid to the follow up and ongoing usage of the ideas presented.

—Diana Williams

Our district afforded us the gift of a professional-development days throughout the school year. For the January professional-development day, our school leadership team decided that the staff wanted ideas to improve student discipline and respect. We reviewed the school-discipline data and decided that several students were frequently in trouble. We called upon Michael Wynn (1993) and his "chickens to eagles" program. At that time, our mascot was a vicious looking wildcat, and the staff had been toying with the idea of changing the mascot to an eagle.

We arranged to have our professional-development day at a hotel site with a continental breakfast and lunch. We had written grants and had staff-development funds to support this effort. This was a perfect time of the year to do this, as there is such a letdown after the winter break, with a long three months of winter facing us in the Midwest. This was a day to reset our agenda, feel like professionals, and tackle our discipline problems.

We had the appointed day with Michael Wynn (1993) based on his book, *The Eagles Who Thought They Were Chickens*. It was a moving day that culminated in everyone making a personal commitment to incorporate some facet of his teaching methods into their classroom practice. He was a very motivational and inspirational speaker. Our intention was

to go back to school and implement some of his strategies for increasing self-respect and self-discipline among our students. One of the closing activities was "How will you take this information and use it back at the building?" We went around the room, and everyone shared the impact the session had on them, and how they intended to use the information. When we got to the art teacher, a person of few words, he stood up and held up the most beautiful sketch of an expansive soaring eagle. We all gasped as he quietly talked about how he would forever more view all students as potential eagles. It was magical.

Later, we all voted to change the mascot to the eagle and launched a campaign with the students to get them to draw sketches, write stories, and discuss attributes of eagles. We implemented a new staff-designed discipline plan encouraging all students to "soar like eagles." I approached the art teacher and asked him if we could commission him to paint the large eagle he had drawn on a large exterior wall of the school. During that summer, he engaged older students from neighboring schools to paint our new mascot, the eagle, on our wall. That professional-development day gave us the shot in the arm to sustain our enthusiasm and excitement throughout those dreary winter months.

My Journal Story

_____

_____

_____

_____

_____

_____

_____

_____

_____

_____

_____

_____

_____

_____

_____

_____

_____

_____

Lessons Learned

- Professional development must be tied to the context of the job-embedded needs for a school staff.

- Sometimes, the quietest person on staff will have the most powerful idea. It is important that every voice is heard. We must intentionally ask for input from everyone.

- Thoughtful planning about the delivery, timing, and process of professional development will assure a successful program.

- It is not enough to have an outstanding professional-development program. Attention must be paid to the follow-up and ongoing usage of the ideas presented.

Mini Coaching

- What guides your collaborative planning for professional development?

- How do you know how well the professional-development ideas are being implemented and what the impact is?

- As you think about needs for professional development for your campus, what data will you use to determine the needs?

- What creative processes can you think of for the delivery of professional development?

Establishing a Norm of Professionalism

Professional development will yield a high return on investment in the form of a high-performance school and high-performing staff members, with subsequent greater benefits for students.

—Diana Williams

We were fortunate at one time in our school district to have professional-development days scheduled throughout the school year and monthly early-dismissal days. Early on, when planning the early-dismissal days, inevitably a teacher would say to me, "Since it is *just* an inservice day, do you mind if I schedule my doctor's appointment for after school and leave early?" To which I would inevitably say, "Our professional-development time is a valuable resource and must be treated as just as important as our regular work day." A few teachers would schedule a personal day off for the professional-development day, again saying, "Since it is *just* a professional-development day, and I don't have kids, it's a good time for me to schedule off."

Part of the issue is that in the early days, "inservice days" were just that—"sit and get" *inservice days.* I can remember being on the provider end of professional development as a staff-development supervisor. Harried principals would call me a few days before a scheduled professional-development day and ask, "What can you do or get for my staff for inservice day?" As a principal, I wanted our professional development to be the professional experience that I had been a proponent of, of a needs-based,

job-embedded opportunity growing out of a collaborative school culture. That's why I was always surprised by staff members who viewed it as down-time to do other things.

As the principal, I took responsibility for trying to shift the old professional-development paradigm into the new paradigm of job-embedded work time to forge a community of learners and leaders. By having ongoing team meetings where we continuously looked at what was happening with our students and what we could do about it, we were able to identify the *content* of our meetings. Teachers shared the ownership of the professional-development days as the *context* for our time to study and learn and plan together. The *process* of professional-development days became natural and ongoing as outgrowths of our continuous work together. We used the *Standards for Professional Development* published by the National Staff Development Council (2001) as a basis for planning our professional development.

I learned that the principal is the principle staff developer and the initial keeper of the vision of a professional learning community. When this vision becomes dim, the opportunity for professional-learning time goes away.

My Journal Story

_____

_____

_____

_____

_____

_____

_____

_____

_____

_____

_____

_____

_____

_____

_____

_____

_____

Lessons Learned

- The principal is the broker of professional-development time and must protect this gift of time for its intended purpose.

- The principal must think of creative ways to etch out professional-development time.

- Professional development will yield a high return on investment in the form of a high-performance school and high-performing staff members, with subsequent greater benefits for students.

Mini Coaching

- What are some ways you etch out time for professional development?

- What kinds of results do you expect from professional development?

- How do you transmit your vision for staff learning and growth to others?

Williams, D. (2008). "Establishing a Norm of Professionalism" originally appeared in the *Principals Office*, an ezine for school administrators from The Ohio State University's P–12 Project and Interprofessional Commission. The *Principal's Office* is available at www.principalsoffice.osu.edu.

Making Time for Professional Development

Schools get better when everyone is a learner and everyone becomes a leader.

—Diana Williams

One of the daunting challenges of providing high-quality professional development is finding the time for staff collaboration. Principals have been innovative and creative in carving out the necessary time for professional development. Some ideas include the following.

> District-sanctioned early dismissals
>
> District-sanctioned professional-development days
>
> Provision of substitutes to release staff
>
> Providing in-school coverage by grouping students for special activities while teachers work together
>
> Use of "specials" to schedule grade-level teachers with common planning time
>
> Use of summer for professional development

At our school, we tried another approach. We were relentless in writing grants to fund our professional learning. We hired a former teacher from our own school who had retired. She came back and subbed for us four days a week. We devised a schedule allowing every teacher to have one half day per month to plan interventions, crunch data, develop lessons aligned with the district curriculum, attend professional-development meetings, go on professional visitations to other programs, and to carry out other professional responsibilities. The good thing about using an excellent retired teacher from the school is that the students knew her, and she knew them. There was continuity in their learning without the usual discipline concerns. Of course, the retired teacher loved coming back to her old school in this capacity and enjoyed the shortened workweek. The teachers kept a log of their activities during their professional-development time. The results of this arrangement were that teachers brought many new ideas to their teaching, they brought suggestions for other professional-development ideas that would help them to help their students, and there was an aura of professionalism and collaboration in the building. Teachers were able to reflect upon and improve their practice. Teachers were far better at analyzing their student data and were far more effective with student assessment and differentiation.

Another nuance of our professional-development process was that if a teacher elected to attend a professional-development conference or training, he or she was then asked to present the material at a subsequent staff meeting or at our summer retreat. For the very first summer retreat we held, several teachers had attended a school team conference earlier in the summer. They knew they would be required to present their respective session information to the rest of the staff. Each one asked for no more than 15 minutes to present. It was soon clear at the retreat that each one needed more time, as they had thoroughly prepared and were genuinely excited about their material. Each one went on much longer than their allotted 15 minutes. At the end of the retreat, one of the suggestions for the future was to "Make the retreat longer. We need more time!"

My Journal Story

_____

_____

_____

_____

_____

_____

_____

_____

_____

_____

_____

_____

_____

_____

_____

_____

_____

_____

_____

_____

_____

_____

_____

Lessons Learned

- I learned that schools get better when everyone is a learner and everyone becomes a leader. Professional-development opportunities provided the mechanism for teachers to be reflective, accountable, and professional.

- Local school sites must be creative in garnering time for professional learning together.

- Teachers enjoy the opportunity to share with each other. It is important to put the structures in place to make this possible.

Mini Coaching

- Think of ways you have extended professional-learning opportunities to your staff. What worked and why?

- How has the professional learning contributed to the academic growth of your students?

- What else are you thinking about for professional learning for your school?

Williams, D. (2008). "Making Time for Professional Development" originally appeared in the *Principals Office,* an ezine for school administrators from The Ohio State University's P–12 Project and Interprofessional Commission. The *Principal's Office* is available at www.principalsoffice.osu.edu.

How Are You Implementing the Professional Learning?

School improvement is most surely and thoroughly achieved when teachers engage in frequent, continuous and increasingly concrete talk about teaching practices . . . capable of distinguishing one practice and it's virtue from another.

—Judith Warren Little, Education Researcher

In a follow-up staff meeting to our conference with Michael Wynn, we looked individually at the ideas we had just heard and then discussed in small groups how we were applying his work to make learning relevant for all of the children. The topic related peripherally to "cultural sensitivity," and some staff members were reluctant to address this issue, while others were adamant that the whole school should participate. I asked the staff to take one of four positions: (1) "I don't get it, and don't understand it," (2) "I get it but don't know how I'll incorporate it into all that I'm already doing," (3) "I get it, and I am using it. I have some questions and would like to know more about how others are using it," and (4) "I'm using it, and these are some ways I'm using it." I then asked them to form groups, making sure there was one person representing each position in each group. The small groups spent the rest of the time sharing points of view and coming to consensus on how they would proceed. We then reported out to the larger group.

This process opened up dialogue for staff members to understand different points of view about the innovation, provided support to those who wanted more information and help, and provided an opportunity for those who embraced the innovation to be leaders of the implementation.

My Journal Story

_____

_____

_____

_____

_____

_____

_____

_____

_____

_____

_____

_____

_____

_____

_____

_____

_____

_____

_____

Lessons Learned

- It is essential to assess how new strategies and programs are being implemented by the staff. Often, it is assumed programs either do or do not work, when in fact the success or failure of a program is related more to the implementation or lack of implementation of the program.

- It is important to give leadership roles to teachers who are able to lead implementation of innovations. They have credibility with other teachers.

- It is equally important to give voice and support to teachers who are struggling with innovations.

Mini Coaching

- What goals do you have for the professional development of your staff?

- How do you model continuous learning for yourself?

- What kind of follow-up activities do you engage in to keep learning ongoing for yourself as well as for staff?

Professional-Development Snippet
Staff Retreat

The key is to replace a belief in "experts" who "deliver" knowledge of what good teaching is to workshops with communities of teachers who learn through ongoing collaboration and practice.

—Dennis Sparks,
National Staff Development Council

A summer retreat with your staff gives a lot of mileage in teambuilding, planning, and setting a tone of high expectations for the new year. The first year I proposed a retreat, it was difficult to get the staff to commit to the idea, but finally 90% of the staff committed to a one-and-a-half-day retreat scheduled at a state park about forty miles away. This included a one-night stay. After the success of the first retreat, the overwhelming comment on the evaluation was that the retreat did not provide enough time. Subsequent retreats were two and one-half days long.

We had aggressively applied for and secured grants, which funded our professional-development work. As the principal, I had high expectations that the staff was and would be treated as professionals and leaders. I expected a high return on the investment in professional development in greater impact and success for our students.

The first step is to get the commitment to participate from the majority of the staff. If a staff is newly formed or has had problems with staff relations, try to get a critical mass of staff members representative of the divisions or cliques within the staff. The results of the retreat will have greater acceptance by all if the participants are not a handpicked group of the principal's favorites. Ask for volunteers to help plan the retreat. Once you have a committee formed, the following tasks need to be accomplished.

Logistics committee: Secure the location, negotiate room rates, and secure a firm commitment to participate from the staff. Set the time frames, select the meals, and write a fun and inviting invitation with the pertinent information on it.

Professional-development committee: Based upon student data, staff surveys, team or grade-level reports, data from your school-improvement plan, or other identified professional-development needs, decide upon a unifying theme for the retreat. We sought "best practices" for one of our retreats. Any staff person who attended a professional-development activity throughout the year was expected to present at the retreat, so certain staff members were predrafted to facilitate or present a segment. We incorporated the school mascot in some way to build team spirit at the retreat. For example, one year, we embraced "Soaring With the Eagles" as a theme for the retreat. In addition, we incorporated school-district goals and requirements into the retreat. One year, the district had introduced a new reading program. We used part of the time to have a district literacy coach come to help us develop our implementation plan. Another year, we had a math literacy person come to help us address one of our math deficiencies on the state test. We paid attention to adult learning and incorporated multiple ways of learning, such as whole-group activities, small-group activities, teambuilding activities, and individual reflection time. We used a variety of media, such as newsprint with colorful markers, art activities, video clips, and manipulatives; and, we had treats!

Extracurricular-activities committee: The retreat usually included pre- and/or post-retreat activities in the event a staff person wanted to include his or her family. Usually, the retreats were held at state parks where there were activities such as hiking, swimming, horseback riding, and a wide variety of other activities. Several staff members brought their families, joining them either prior to the retreat or after the retreat for an extended vacation.

In addition to extended planning opportunities for family members, the committee arranged fun, extracurricular activities for the staff. Usually, we would gather in the evenings for games, group hikes, scavenger hunts, or whatever else the committee came up with. We learned to play together as well as work together. The whole process built the team and fostered a positive school culture that carried over beyond the retreat.

Following is a sample agenda for a one-and-a-half-day retreat:

Day 1

Setting: A state park lodge 30 to 60 minutes driving distance

12:00–1:30 p.m.: Staff arrival, check in, and luncheon.

1:30–2:00: Finish checking in and assemble in meeting room.

2:00–3:00: Teambuilding Activity, "Celebrating Our Successes." Everyone write a story about a student or family situation wherein you know for a fact you were successful. Use a marker, and put it on a 4" × 24" strip of colored construction paper. During the retreat, take time to have different members share their stories. Post the strips in a starburst design on the wall of the meeting room to acknowledge and celebrate your collective successes. Ask them to take the strips back to school with them and revisit their stories when they have a particularly difficult day or student.

3:00–5:00: Developing the "big ideas" to work on. Brainstorm for 20 minutes on "What we've done well this past year." Post these results on newsprint on walls. Brainstorm for 20 minutes on "What we'd like to improve upon this new year." Post the results on newsprint. Pass out five sticky dots to each member. Let each

member choose the top-five areas that they would like to see addressed in the upcoming year. (You may pass out three dots if your staff is small.) Put the dots next to your five votes. These become your priority areas to work on. Now, write the five priority areas each at the top of a clean piece of chart paper, and post these around the room. Ask everyone to sign up for one to three areas to work on (again, depending on the size of your group). The top name on each chart will be the "point person" for that topic. No one person should be the point person for more than one topic. The last several minutes should be spent with each group collectively deciding where they will begin their "committee" work the next morning. In a park setting, groups may take their newsprint to a comfortable location in the lodge to work on their plan. They should come back with (1) what should be done about this topic (strategies), (2) when it should be done (timeline), (3) who will carry out the plan (who will make up the work team to carry it out), and (4) what criteria will show the plan is successful (evaluation of project).

5:00–5:30: Break.

5:30–6:30: Candlelight dinner together.

6:30–8:30: Inspiring educational movie, popcorn, pop, and discussion, such as *The Freedom Writers* (LaGravanese, DeVito, Shamberg, & Sher, 2007). You may develop a movie guide with pertinent questions for discussion, or you may conduct an open-ended discussion.

8:30–10:00: Socializing.

Day 2

8:00–8:30 a.m.: Continental breakfast.

8:30–10:00: Committee work at locations decided upon by the groups.

10:00–10:30: Break.

10:30–12:00 p.m.: Committee reports and plans. The whole group refines and responds to the reports. When finished, you will have assignments, timelines, and promising strategies to address improvements for your school.

12:00–1:00: Luncheon and check out.

1:00–3:00: Staff professional development—this is an opportunity to have staff members who have developed good ideas throughout the school year or who have attended professional-development conferences to share new information with their colleagues. It was my experience that while staff members may have been reluctant to "present" to their peers initially, they were well prepared and actually needed more time for their topics. Presenting to each other keeps them engaged and spreads the positive effects of what each had learned.

3:00–3:15: Short break.

3:15–5:15: Staff professional development Part II—this is an opportunity to bring in an outside resource, to present new information from the district, or present promising practices that you are interested in, or in having more of your staff members present. Save administrivia for newsletters and bulletins back at the building!

5:15–6:15: Celebration dinner. Make it fun and festive! Celebrate the fun things that have happened during the retreat, give fun awards to each person: certificates and small gifts or professional books. Everyone will go off on a high note.

Once the retreat is over and everyone returns to school, be intentional about carrying the hard work undertaken at the retreat back to your building. Staff members will have committed to carrying out plans and serving on committees. Monitor the committee work, and celebrate accomplishments. The students and parents will recognize a renewed vibrancy in the climate as the staff works together to implement plans.

Other suggestions for creating time for professional development include

Planning summer retreats for concentrated planning and meeting time;

Hiring retired teachers from your own building to become regular professional-development substitutes—this provides continuity for students and their learning;

Utilizing all time provided by the district for professional development; allowing this time to be eroded by teachers taking time off for appointments or to do regular work in their classrooms will result in the loss of this valuable resource;

Making sure you follow the contractual protocols for "changing working conditions" if your school is unionized; get buy in and a sign off for all who are affected by changes;

Trusting teachers to get the work accomplished; they can be creative in carving out their own time if there is sufficient ownership and rationale for the work; and

Following all rules regarding the supervision of students; have appropriate school personnel accountable for students at all times, and follow all rules and policies in your district regarding the use of volunteers.

Williams, D. (2008). "Staff Retreat" originally appeared in the *Principals Office,* an ezine for school administrators from The Ohio State University's P–12 Project and Interprofessional Commission. The *Principal's Office* is available at www.principalsoffice.osu.edu.

Our Principal,

*She likes to make sure that kids
don't get hurt.*

She loves it when kids give her pictures.

She likes it when kids read to her.

Tara

CHAPTER

Standard Three

A school administrator is an educational leader who promotes the success of all students by ensuring management of the organization, operations, and resources for a safe, efficient, and effective learning environment.

MANAGING AN EFFECTIVE ORGANIZATION

INTRODUCTION
Good Management = An Effective Learning Environment

In promoting the success for all students, what are the elements or parts that make this happen in an ordinary school on an ordinary day when you may or may not be concentrating on theory or the last principals' meeting, but you are fully focused on creating a positive learning climate that supports student learning? In answering this question, you are invited to join me for part of my routine day.

The meeting with the grade-level chairpersons has just ended; we discussed where and how the soon-to-be delivered, new, hands-on science equipment would be stored and made accessible to each teacher, as there is no common space available for storage; a decision was reached: Each chairperson would be responsible for the storage and dissemination of science materials when needed. The school day has started, and it is now time to visit some classrooms. Today, I am going to focus on how well the students are attending to the teacher and their work. During my training to become an elementary principal, one of my professors had a favorite idiom when talking about the duties and responsibilities of the principal, which was "shirt-sleeve leadership." This phrase has stuck with me through the years; it is the concept of providing supervision while walking around. With those words floating around in my head, the daily journey through the building has started as I walk in and out of classrooms, observing the looks on the faces of the students; the teaching styles of the teachers; the number of students who are engaged in their lessons; the teachers' management styles; the lesson-plan books; student work; the content of the walls; and even seemingly insignificant things, such as the teacher using a chalkboard that has

been used repeatedly without washing, so the work being written on the board blends in with the chalk dust of the past; but also the teacher who is teaching a social studies lesson and has the students so fired up they are literally hopping out of their seats, wanting to participate—which makes me want to respond or stay around a little longer. Through this process, information is gathered that can be used to make informed decisions about what is needed to promote the success of all students and whether there is congruence between what is taught and the standards established by the school district and state. The informal observations also serve as vehicles for discussing teaching and learning with individual teachers.

Back in my office, I open up the notebook containing test scores from the previous year; we are not privileged to have short-cycle testing data, so I have to rely on information that was collected at the end of the last school year and previous years. I look for trends; are there certain patterns that glare like the brilliance of an intense sun? I have determined that strengths and weaknesses of our school can be gleaned from the performance of certain teachers' classes, groups of students, individual students, and grade levels. After examining test data, I find myself plowing through the mounds of progress reports that have been sent to the office for my perusal before being sent home. It is important that information coming from the school is able to pass the same litmus test used to assess the work of students—spelling, grammar, grading practices, neatness in presentation, and notes to parents that are tactfully written. The number of errors is usually small but significant enough to spend the time needed to continue the practice. This teacher behavior does not occur now (I hope), but I had one teacher who was vindictive in grading students. Those who posed severe behavior problems during the school year were retained, although there was enough evidence to substantiate passing them on to the next grade—this practice was desisted. On the other end of the continuum, you might have a teacher that is too benevolent to give a failing grade. Our school district developed a policy that eliminated the use of minuses when giving *Outstanding*, *Satisfactory*, *Improvement needed*, and *Unsuccessful* grades, but I discovered that some teachers were so attached to the minus symbol that they continued using them. Fortunately, confronting a lack of conformity can produce amazingly positive results. Plans are underway for a staff retreat, and the information obtained from the summarized data will be used to help make informed decisions about professional-development activities.

There are phone calls to return and school mail to be read, but it is now time to head for the lunchroom and playground. Before I go to those areas, it is necessary to check the halls to ensure the boxes that were delivered during the earlier part of the morning have been cleared and that there are no obstructions in the hallways. A quick glance out of the window tells me that it is okay to have outdoor recess. In some schools, the educational assistants and volunteers supervise the playground, with a teacher on call; but in our school, the teachers provided direct supervision. This was a decision that the staff supported; for whatever reason, the teaching staff appeared to have a more positive influence on student behavior. The custodian and physical-education teacher assume responsibilities for daily checking the playground for debris and inspecting equipment on a regular basis; in the morning, our custodian attaches the removal basketball rims and detaches them in the afternoon—permanent rims in this school community are stolen as soon as they are replaced. Oh, I forgot to check with the school nurse about when the school's "head check" is going to happen. Schoolwide head checks are conducted twice a year, in the fall and in the spring. We have a problem with lice, and checking the heads of our students helps to reduce its spread and to keep our students in school. After a walk in the lunchroom, I must go to the library for a luncheon meeting with our school's student mediators; they are trained to help resolve conflict among the students on the playground. The student-mediation program has worked to help our school obtain a more peaceful playground.

The principal assumes responsibility for the academic success of all students by managing and bringing together all the factors that impact achievement. In reflecting on just part of this ordinary day, one can see how standard three of the ISLLC standards is evident. There are implications of organization, operations, use of resources, and concern for safety. In a school day, no day is ever ordinary because schools are very complex places that require principals to blend vision, creativity, and knowledge with skills that include people skills, managing, supervising, communicating, and decision making. Principals must also be proactive rather than reactive in their efforts to keep schools focused on the main thing, which is teaching and learning and making every day extraordinary.

The Crisis That Wasn't

Some events are just funny. It is good to laugh at the ridiculous.

—Diana Williams

One day, an older gentleman wandered into the building from off of the street. This was before schools routinely locked their doors for safety. He came into the office, making inquiries about the school program. I spoke with him and tried to answer his questions. Then, he lapsed into a monologue of mutters and incoherent statements to himself. It became clear to me that he was suffering from some kind of dementia. When I was unable to get him to leave the building, I signaled the secretary to call security to come and escort him out. He became somewhat belligerent and more agitated, so I closed the office door to keep children and teachers out of the office until we could resolve the situation. I calmly continued to keep him engaged until security could arrive.

About that time, one of the teachers came to the door to come into the office, and I shooed her away with a hand motion. I made the mistake of mouthing to her that it was a "Mrs. Robinson" situation. *Mrs. Robinson* was our code for an intruder. The plan, of course, when these words were mentioned in any context, was that whoever heard the code would pass the word quickly and lock down the building.

Security came and took our "intruder" away to the mental health facility. The secretary and I congratulated ourselves on containing a potentially volatile situation. Meanwhile, we noticed how quiet the building was and that no one had called the office or come to the office in awhile. I looked down the halls, and then it hit me! The building was totally locked down! Doors were locked, and lights were out. Students were hidden in coat closets and under desks.

This situation had caused an unintentional lockdown, but we all congratulated ourselves that our plan worked. We laughed about it later and counted it as our crisis-plan drill for the month.

The lesson learned was that you never know how a situation will present itself. The quick-thinking teacher grasped the situation and acted. We were well prepared and ready.

My Journal Story

- When you plan carefully and everyone is a part of the plan, it will have a better chance of being carried out. We had spent several meetings working out the details for our safety plan, and it worked!

- We must be mindful of the impact our words have on others—either intended or unintended.

- Some events are just funny. It is good to laugh at the ridiculous.

- You never know how a situation will present itself. The key is to be empowered to think and calmly act on the plan.

Mini Coaching

- When have you been confronted with a potentially dangerous situation?

- How did you react?

- What would you do differently next time?

- What additional resources would you like to have in the event a similar situation should occur?

Williams, D. (2008). "The Crisis That Wasn't" originally appeared in the *Principals Office,* an ezine for school administrators from The Ohio State University's P–12 Project and Interprofessional Commission. The *Principal's Office* is available at www.principalsoffice.osu.edu.

Po' Miz Carter

He who cannot dance claims the floor is uneven.

—Hindu Proverb

Mrs. Perkins, the PTA president, entered the building and joined me as I monitored the halls, through which several groups of students were passing on their way back to their classrooms. She glanced up and saw Mrs. Carter and her class as they approached their classroom door and commented on the noise level as well as the somewhat raucous behavior of some of the students. She shared with me that this was the worse class Mrs. Carter had ever tried to teach and that the children should be removed from the school until the parents could change their behavior. "Po' Miz Carter, how could you ever expect her to teach under those circumstances?" That was certainly an excellent question. Usually,

I'm not at a loss for words, but I was caught totally off guard. How do you respond to a belief from a parent who exonerates the teacher from the responsibility of managing his or her class? Suddenly, I had the dual responsibility of being truthful and to guard against saying anything about a staff member that might be considered inflammatory or a defamation of character. I chose to use humor to defuse the situation by stating that it would be a little impossible to keep the students home that long, and they might grow to like it better than school. I also indicated that, as a staff, we should work on improving our management techniques as well as improving the behavior of all our students.

My Journal Story

Lessons Learned

- Lessons can be learned through informal conversations.
- Parents deserve a response when issues are raised.
- Diplomacy must be employed in difficult situations.
- The school and its staff influence parents' perceptions.

Mini Coaching

- How can you help teachers become aware of the impact of their conversations with parents?
- How do you use information obtained from parents?
- What strategies would you use to facilitate change in teacher behavior?
- How will you know when you are successful?

Trapped

In order to transform schools successfully, educators need to navigate the difficult space between letting go of old patterns and grabbing on to new ones.

—Deal 1990 (www.leading-learning.co.nz)

"Good morning, I'm the cadet principal (leadership trainee) that is assigned here for the next couple of days," I announced to the secretary. She looked up, introduced herself, and led me into Mr. Edwards' office. After looking around for a few moments, I decided I needed more information, so I approached her again to request a handbook, the building map, teacher roster, bell schedule, and other pertinent information that would facilitate my coverage of the building during the principal's absence. Mrs. Hoover gathered the necessary documents, gave them to me, and returned to her work. About three days later, I received a call that said the principal was not returning and that I would be assigned to that school for the reminder of the year. With this news, it was time to assume the role of the principal, the one in charge, the decision maker. In preparation for my new job, I needed to determine how the staff viewed the principal and what the expectations of the principal's office entailed. I soon learned that my job description was to count the money in preparation for the school treasurer, fill the pop machine, supervise the lunchroom, and provide the strong arm of discipline. There was no hint of seeing the principal as the instructional leader. Considering the fact that I knew very little about the school and its community, I basically followed the pattern that had been established by the former administrator.

Engaging in activities that interfered with my ability to take care of instructional duties soon became frustrating and intolerable. My first small step was to remove myself from lunchroom duty by developing a duty roster with teachers assigned to the lunchroom. The teachers were not pleased, and I immediately lost favor with those who were the most negligent in their behaviors. During the noon hour, I was "trapped" in the lunchroom and was not able to monitor student or teacher behavior. Our challenging student population required the staff to be and do what it needed to do with full expediency. I had to deal with several discipline problems each day that related to some type of playground altercation. I asked myself how it would be best to improve playground supervision, and the only way to get the answer was to be on the playground. Some of the things that I discovered were teachers

- Reporting late to playground duty;
- Engaging in conversation with each other or the educational assistant; and
- Remaining in one spot and not moving around the area.

Once my visibility increased and I addressed those issues related to supervising the playground, discipline problems decreased. I assigned filling the pop machine and counting the money to other staff members.

My Journal Story

_____

_____

_____

_____

_____

_____

_____

_____

_____

_____

_____

_____

_____

_____

_____

_____

_____

Lessons Learned

- It is necessary to identify those things that interfere with teaching and learning.

- Often, the changes that need to be made are not those that the school staff desires, and you must have the wisdom and courage to do what's best for students.

- Situations often call for reenergizing the staff by helping them to focus on the achievement of their students rather than themselves.

- It is important to seek to remedy a situation as opposed to seeking to blame.

Mini Coaching

- How do you define your leadership role?

- If you had a magic wand, what would your school community look like?

- How will you know when your school community is how you want it to be?

Don't Put Me in the Garbage!

Children do not extract meaning from what they hear others saying; they try instead to relate what has been said to what is going on.

—Judith M. Newman, Editor

All was well when suddenly Mrs. Noon swooped briskly into the office escorting a small, upset kindergarten child by his arm. As I glanced up, she began blurting out, "This child has diarrhea," which was quite obvious as the discharge oozed out from beneath his pant leg, swirled over his shoe top, and headed for the floor. It was time for crisis intervention. We had several concurring problems: a sick child, an upset teacher, and a clean up. I summoned the secretary and requested that she bring me a large garbage bag from the supply closet and contact the parents immediately. The secretary quickly got the bag, handed it to me, and went about the business of trying to make the necessary call. With the bag firmly in hand, I approached the child and he began to scream, "Don't put me in the garbage!" I was jolted suddenly into reality.

I had not shared my intentions with the child, and he stopped fretting over his predicament long enough to express his perceptions of what was happening. I gently placed my hand on his small shoulder and reassured him that he was not going to be thrown into the garbage. To quickly send the message of what I needed for him to do, I decided to demonstrate the behavior that I wanted him to mimic. I stepped into the bag and slightly pulled it up toward the waist and explained how it could be used to make him feel more comfortable until his parents came to take him home. The father of the child arrived, signed little Donnie out, picked him up with bag, and started walking down the street toward their home. Once the child had received the necessary attention, the other problems were easily resolved.

My Journal Story

_____

_____

_____

_____

_____

_____

_____

_____

_____

_____

_____

_____

_____

_____

_____

_____

_____

_____

_____

Lessons Learned

- When working with others, it is impossible for them to know what your intentions are without some explanation.

- It is very necessary to demonstrate sensitivity to the feelings of others, who may be in a challenging position.

- It is important to develop a deep understanding of how children think and interpret their world.

Mini Coaching

- How do you resolve emergencies?

- How do you handle insensitive behavior toward children on the part of adults?

- What resources does your school have on hand to take care of emergencies?

Always Have a Backup Plan!

Always have a Plan A, a Plan B, and sometimes it doesn't hurt to have a Plan C when planning events.

—Diana Williams

This time of the year always reminds me of my first assignment as principal of a large old elementary school. I was able to work with the staff over the summer to determine that we wanted to make a big push for parent involvement. To that end, we decided that we would invite parents to come to school with their children the first day and line up with them on the playground, be greeted by the teacher, and proceed to the classrooms with their children's class lines. After arriving in the classroom and feeling comfortable that their children were settled in, the parents would "be excused" to go to the library to have cookies and coffee and meet the new principal.

Our big day came. All of the class lists were posted over bright, newly painted room numbers on the playground. And then the unexpected happened. It poured buckets of rain just as parents and students were coming to school. Instead of following our well-planned directions, parents and kids were running into the building through every doorway, asking where to go, where was their room, and jamming the office and hallway. I finally came to my senses and over the intercom asked everyone to report to the gym, where we carried out our plan—slightly modified—as teachers met their classes, and parents and took their children to the classrooms.

I've never forgotten this experience. It taught me to always have a backup plan—even for the best-laid plans of a principal.

My Journal Story

_____

_____

_____

_____

_____

_____

_____

_____

_____

_____

_____

_____

_____

_____

_____

_____

_____

_____

_____

Lessons Learned

- Always have a Plan A, a Plan B, and sometimes it doesn't hurt to have a Plan C when planning events.

- Make sure all parties are involved and well informed of the plans and the contingencies.

- When things go wrong, stay calm, and elicit the help of others.

- People are human and will assist when you communicate the problem, accept responsibility, and move on with a new plan when things go wrong.

- It's OK to laugh at yourself after the crisis has passed. Don't take yourself too seriously.

- Learn from your mistakes!

Mini Coaching

- Think of a time when things that you have planned have gone wrong.

- What could you have done differently?

- What did you learn from the experience?

- How do you think about it when you think of it now?

Williams, D. (2008). "Always Have a Backup Plan" originally appeared in the _Principals Office,_ an ezine for school administrators from The Ohio State University's P–12 Project and Interprofessional Commission. The _Principal's Office_ is available at www.principalsoffice.osu.edu.

Cut the Telephone Calls

There is always a time to make right what is wrong.

—Susan Griffin, Author

Thomas Jones, who just returned to the teaching profession after being away for the past several years pursuing a career in the business world, was assigned to our school. He was charming, handsome, and appeared to be enthusiastic about being part of our staff. Within a few days of our initial meeting, he inquired about our fund-raising efforts and volunteered to take over those responsibilities. One can only imagine how delighted I would have been to have a responsible staff member assume such time-consuming and noninstructional activities. My first inclination was to leap to the other side of the desk and embrace him, but then I reasoned that this type of behavior was not appropriate as well as my intuition seemed to caution me about the motives of this staff member. I "thanked him" profusely for offering that "wonderful act of kindness" and his desire to contribute to the successful operation of our school, and I explained to him that our general fund instructional assistant organized and monitored our fundraisers.

Mr. Jones readily became part of our school and community. He used his personal attributes to win favor with the female staff members and a particular "mom" who had a child in his room. As I walked through the building, I began to notice things that appeared to be out of the norm, such as a female teacher staying around the building later than usual in the company of Mr. Jones, or a parent who dramatically increased her amount of parent involvement or parent presence in his classroom. After a couple of months passed, the secretary, who had not succumbed to his charm, informed me about the exceptional number and nature of telephone calls he received and that she was asked to immediately inform him about such calls. Since school secretaries in most elementary schools are overworked—that certainly could be said of ours—she was not going to assume an additional responsibility that had not been directed by me. The upstairs telephone, located in an area adjacent to the Title I reading-teacher's room, had to be accessed by passing through her space, which disturbed the students. The privacy was limited and conversations were easily overheard. The reading teacher became concerned about the regularity of his intrusions and the content of the calls, which had nothing to do with school. She shared her concerns with me.

The information regarding the telephone situation was probably accurate and needed to be corrected, but it was not something that I personally witnessed. The most expedient method of resolving the problem, for me, was to be matter-of-fact and address the issue through the daily bulletin. I reminded the staff about the written policy in the teachers' handbook regarding the use of school telephones and how incoming messages were to be handled: The secretary would take messages from all callers and place them in the teachers' mailboxes—unless it was an emergency—so please remember to check them. The decision that I made to bring attention to this policy and its implementation resolved the problem for the secretary and the Title I teacher, exonerated their involvement, and treated the situation as a general concern, but it created a wedge between me and Mr. Jones.

My Journal Story

Lessons Learned

- Problems need to be resolved in the most professional and least controversial manner.

- It is important to keep the trust of those who confide in you.

- It is important to trust your own intuition and to be observant.

Mini Coaching

- When have you resolved an issue that was shared with you privately?

- How can you maintain the integrity of those who share information with you?

- What are multiple ways of resolving staff-initiated concerns?

Are We the Good Kids or the Bad?

One way to change people is to see them differently.

—Barry Stevens, Author

As our discipline committee tried to devise creative solutions to improving the discipline of our students, someone came up with the idea to do a "discipline survey" with a representative group of students. We wanted to know what made them tick and what kinds of incentives and consequences would work best with them. We identified a "good citizen" type from each classroom to participate in the discipline survey. I thought we should include a few of the students who were always in trouble as well, so each teacher identified one of these students. I decided to conduct the survey in a focus-group format. Our paraprofessional discipline assistant took the notes as I facilitated the discussion. The questions included

1. What is the thing you like best about school?

2. What is your least favorite thing about school?

3. What kinds of rewards would you like to see for good behavior?

4. What kinds of consequences should there be for students who break the rules?

5. What other ideas do you have for making our school a better school?

We divided the students into small groups for the focus groups. At the first focus group, after assembling the students in a circle on chairs, I could see some of the students nervously looking around at who was in the group. Finally, one of our more mischievous persons asked, "Hey, are we the good kids or the bad kids?" I said, "You have each been asked to be in this group because of your 'leadership' skills. We know you are ready to stand up and help your school become a better place." They seemed satisfied with that answer, and we all went about the work of making our school that better place.

My Journal Story

_____

_____

_____

_____

_____

_____

_____

_____

_____

_____

_____

_____

_____

_____

_____

_____

_____

_____

_____

Lessons Learned

- I should not have been surprised at how perceptive students are about their rank or status in school. They have well-formed perceptions of whom they are and what role they play.

- I learned that one of the greatest challenges that we have is to help students develop a sense of the greater possibilities of who they are and can be.

- It is important to include students in assessing the needs of your school. They bring broad and unique insights.

- As adults, we can model and teach collaborative, problem-solving processes for our students.

Mini Coaching

- In what ways do you model collaborative processes for your students and staff?

- What processes do you have in place for students to contribute to discipline and climate issues in the school?

- Think of a time when you were in a school setting with a positive school climate. What made the climate positive and conducive to student learning?

- What do you want for your students?

The Battle Is Lost

'Tis Education forms the common mind, Just as the Twig Is bent, the Tree's inclin'd.

—Alexander Pope

There are some students that are so unforgettable; they remain part of your memory throughout the years. Tony is one of those students. He was an attractive five-year-old kindergartener who probably looked like an angel as he slept; but once awake, any resemblance to a celestial being was not to be found, at least during the school day when he was in 3D mode—decry, defy, or destroy: Tony would loudly verbalize his desire to not cooperate, take advantage of any opportunity to defy authority, and destroy items or projects that belonged to others. Techniques used by the classroom teacher to quench the undesirable behavior were of no avail, and as a final consequence, on several occasions, Tony was sent to the office, where a magical transformation would occur. It happened only when he was the focal point of my attention, which kept me fully engaged with him. His mother had come to the school for conferences about her son, and she seemed convinced that we were the ones with the problem. On this particular day when the office magic was not too effective, I chose to take Tony home rather than call his mother to come get him. Fortunately for me, the mother opened the door and I was able to enter the house to explain the circumstances surrounding the visit. While I was sharing my story, a miracle happened; Tony apparently became bored, climbed upon a chair and onto the dining room table, walked across it, and ignored his mother's pleas to get down. Finally, she was able to subdue him, and I decided it was time for mother and son to have their privacy, so I established a conference time for the next day and returned to school.

The following morning upon arriving at school, Tony was sent to his classroom and a conference was held with his mother about his behavior. She seemed to be more willing to listen, less defensive, and admitted that Tony's behavior surfaced in places other than school. We concluded our conference with a plan of action that included (1) taking him to a doctor for a physical assessment, (2) the mother obtaining information on and enrolling in parenting classes, and (3) a timeline denoting when these activities would occur. Tony was diagnosed as hyperactive by his pediatrician and placed on medication, which modified his behavior at school. As is the case with so many young people that attended our school, the family moved, and the long-term results of our hard work were not known.

My Journal Story

- Sometimes, it is necessary to lose the battle in order to win the war.

- Knowledge about the whole child enables one to understand the challenges that might be faced and provides guidance in choosing the appropriate solution to a problem.

- Trust is important in establishing a relationship that yields results.

- Home visits can be very informative and productive.

Mini Coaching

- Describe the behaviors that you would like to see exhibited by a child that challenges authority.

- What resources could you use to help mediate the problems that a student might be experiencing?

- In what ways do you mediate differences in points of view about discipline?

Extinguishing Poor Behavior

It is important not to let children push our buttons. When they do, we often sink to childlike behavior ourselves rather than maintaining our professionalism.

—Diana Williams

One day, one of the first-grade teachers marched Freddie up from her room on the lower level to my office. She was visibly shaken, exclaiming, "He won't stop whistling. He won't stop whistling. He won't stop whistling!" Obviously, the student had really gotten to her, and she was about to blow her cool. Apologetically, she said she had tried everything, but that he just kept whistling, and she could not stand it any longer. I calmly said to them, "You know, I have been rather lonely and bored this morning. I could use someone to cheer me up. Freddie, why don't you stay here with me and entertain me with your whistling?" The teacher looked at me rather quizzically, but I assured her that we would be fine and that she should return to her class. She left Freddie with me, and I politely asked him to have a seat at my table and to whistle for me. He began to whistle, and I watched him for a few seconds then said, "That's just what I've needed down here in this lonely office." I said, "Continue." He seemed delighted to comply. I continued the report I had been doing on the computer. Shortly, I noticed Freddie stopped whistling, so I said, "Oh please don't stop. I am enjoying your music so much." Again, he happily obliged me, and again he stopped after awhile. We went through this sequence several times with Freddie growing more weary of whistling without the pleasure of an attentive audience. Finally, he asked if he could return to his room. I said I was enjoying his whistling too much. So, we resumed this pattern for a few more rounds. Again, he asked if he could return to his room. I reluctantly reasoned with him that while I knew he was really missing out on the fun in his room, I was really going to miss him whistling to me. I told him if he got the urge to whistle again, my door would always be open to him to come and whistle for me. I escorted him back to class. The teacher was composed and met us at the door. I told her in front of him that I was reluctantly returning him to class and that I had thoroughly enjoyed his whistling to me. And, should he ever want to whistle again, to send him back to me. He couldn't get to his seat fast enough. Later, the teacher said he had not whistled anymore and asked me what I had done to him. I replied that somewhere out of my behavioral psychology I had remembered the term, "extinguishing undesirable behavior!" In this technique, you repeat the behavior so much that it loses its appeal as a stimulus. He never whistled in class again.

My Journal Story

_____

_____

_____

_____

_____

_____

_____

_____

_____

_____

_____

_____

_____

_____

_____

_____

_____

_____

_____

Lessons Learned

- It is important to be creative in handling children. Children respond to creative solutions rather than a one-size-fits-all approach.

- It is helpful to review theories of child development and to employ age-appropriate strategies.

- It is important not to let children push our buttons. When they do, we often sink to childlike behavior ourselves rather than maintaining our professionalism.

- It is not necessary to yell and scream at children or to use harsh punishments to obtain their compliance. A child having to deal with the logical consequence of their action is a much more meaningful lesson for life.

Mini Coaching

- Think of a time that you have had a successful outcome in working with an unruly child. What did you do to make the outcome successful?

- What other successful discipline strategies have you used with students?

- How have you been able to help your staff with creative ways to work with unruly students?

Tell Your Mother What You Did

It is important to have several layers of corrective behavior in order to give students many legal options for due process.

—Diana Williams

By the time students came to me for disciplinary reasons, they had worked themselves through our staff-designed discipline plan with various tiers of consequences administered by the classroom teacher. The last step a teacher would take would be to send a student to the PEAK (positive experiences and knowledge) room. We were fortunate to have this time-out room called PEAK, staffed by a specially trained, very competent, and caring paraprofessional. The idea of this program in our school district was to keep kids engaged in their schoolwork even when they had to be removed temporarily from their classrooms. They were also able to work out a behavior contract with the paraprofessional. If there were further violations, students found themselves in the office to see me, the principal.

Once I had established rapport with parents in my school, I generally liked to maintain contact with them both to report good things that were happening and to keep them informed about the behavioral incidents that occurred in school. We had a formal process to notify parents of a PEAK referral or a suspension; however, in addition to these formal processes, I liked to have personal contact with the parents when possible. When confronted with an unruly student, I would dial the home number or the number on file. When I reached the parent or guardian, I'd say, "Hello, this is Dr. Williams. Your child is alright—he's not sick or injured, but we've had a problem today that he'd like to tell you about." Then, I would hand the phone to the student, who I would have standing next to me. I'd say, "Tell your mother or father what you did." Usually, the student would begin to make an excuse or tell what another child had done. I would gently say, "Tell her what you did." Then, the story would tumble out. The reactions on the other end of the line ranged from the parent saying, "I'll see you when you get home!" to those that questioned or counseled the child on the spot. Usually, the parent would want to talk to me again, and he or she would thank me for calling, pledging to talk to the child again when the student got home. Occasionally, a parent would try to defensively elicit further details from me, but I would always refer back to what the child had just told them and make them aware of any additional pending action. Upon hanging up the phone, I would reiterate to the student what the parent had said to me and let the student know that his or her parents and I were on the same page. I found this to be a very effective strategy to improve the behavior of unruly children and to develop partnerships with parents and guardians.

My Journal Story

_____

_____

_____

_____

_____

_____

_____

_____

_____

_____

_____

_____

_____

_____

_____

_____

_____

Lessons Learned

- It is important to develop rapport with parents by communicating positive information about their children—as well as the negative.

- As it is natural for children to blame someone or something else when there is an incident, it is helpful to have them tell "what they did" rather than having an adult tell them what they did. It helps children to be accountable for their behaviors and acknowledge their part in the situation.

- Parents like to be informed in a timely way. Often, there is anger when parents find out much later that there has been a problem.

- It is important to have several layers of corrective behavior in order to give students many legal options for due process.

Mini Coaching

- What are your beliefs about child development and student discipline? What additional skills do you want to develop?

- What kind of discipline plan is your total staff engaged in? What is your vision of a safe and orderly climate in your school?

- What are some ways you'd like to develop rapport and effective communication with parents?

- What successes have you had in turning an unruly child around?

A Time for Office Discipline

The office zone developed into a problem-solving space rather than a free-for-all discipline arena.

—Diana Williams

Prior to establishing a schoolwide discipline plan, there were certain times of the month—for example, just before holidays or during a full moon, it seems, and on Friday afternoons—when the students just got wild. Teachers, at their wit's end, would send students to the office at all times during the day. Exasperated, I'd have them sit in the office until I could get to them, counsel with them, and then send them back to class. It was this chaos in the office that prompted a problem-solving session with the staff to form a discipline plan and an orderly way of dealing with unruly students. Everyone agreed that it did no one any good having kids lined up in the office to "see the principal."

In addition to developing "tiered" consequences for each classroom, we strengthened the process for sending students to in-school suspension. The final step was that students would come to see the principal. Once students were assigned to me, the solution became mine and teachers began to accept and look forward to my creative, quirky sessions with students. We established the last recess period of the day for me to see students. This was the only time students were sitting in the office for corrective measures, and they sat there on their free time.

While they awaited their turn to speak to the principal, I had them fill out a form loosely based on William Glasser's (1975) work, which asked the following four questions:

1. Why are you here? Please tell what your part was in this.

2. What were the results of your actions?

3. What would you do differently next time?

4. What is your plan for correcting this situation?

The last section had room for "principal's notes": I was able to note the outcome of our session and any other notes. I kept these forms on file in case I wanted to speak to a parent about the situation, or the teacher wanted additional information. I was also able to reference these notes if a student was a repeat offender.

My Journal Story

_____

_____

_____

_____

_____

_____

_____

_____

_____

_____

_____

_____

_____

_____

_____

_____

_____

Lessons Learned

- The teachers took pride in being able to handle their own discipline problems with an agreed-upon, tiered approach that they developed.

- The teachers also took pride in the office being an orderly, businesslike area.

- The students became accustomed to the procedures for handling discipline, which cut down the time they spent denying or trying to get out of going to the office.

- The office zone developed into a problem-solving space rather than a free-for-all discipline arena, which it had sometimes been in the past.

Mini Coaching

- What areas of student management have you been considering for improvement?

- How have you involved the staff in developing procedures for student management?

- How does your office zone present to the community?

- Are there other areas of management that you would like to work on?

The Graffiti Story

The principal sets the tone for how high the expectations are for staff, community, and students. All will rise to meet the bar if it is set high enough.

—Diana Williams

In the first week of school in my new assignment, I found the concrete "tunnels" play apparatus on the playground to be targets for vandals. They spray painted graffiti on them about every other night. Each day we showed up at school, it was heartbreaking to see our beautiful playground trashed, but I would instruct the custodial staff each day to paint over the mess. At first there were excuses that we did not have the right kind of paint. Eventually, the custodian questioned the decision to continue painting over the graffiti because as he stated, "They were just going to keep doing it!" I made it clear that I didn't care what it took; the graffiti was going to be removed. Vandalism to our property was a nonnegotiable. So, the custodial staff undertook the task and dutifully covered the tunnels each day they were trashed.

I chided the vandals in our school newsletter and appealed to our community to watch out for our school and to keep it beautiful for our students. I don't know what the magic bullet was, but the vandalism eventually stopped. We were subsequently able to put a garden and new signage on the property. These improvements and the tunnels were never disturbed again.

My Journal Story

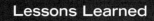

Lessons Learned

- The principal sets the tone for how high the expectations are for staff, community, and students. All will rise to meet the bar if it is set high enough.

- The community can be a powerful ally in helping to monitor the school grounds.

- The custodial staff responded to firm and determined leadership.

Mini Coaching

- Think about a time when you had to assert your leadership for a principle you believed in with a staff member. What made the staff member respect your point of view?

- What steps can you take to stand up to a difficult staff member?

- If your school has been the victim of vandalism, how did you put a stop to it?

- What other ideas do you have?

The Principal Always Rings the Bell

More heads are more thoughtful about a situation than one.

—Diana Williams

Shortly after arriving at my new assignment, I was sitting in my office one stormy morning when the kindergarten teacher popped her head in and inquired, "Are we going to have outside recess?" I looked up from my work and looked from the teacher to the window and said, "It's raining." She added sheepishly, "The other principals always rang the bell to tell us if we should stay inside or go outside." I told her I would do it on that day since it "had always been done that way," but that we'd bring it up as an agenda item at the next meeting.

At the next staff meeting, I brought up the fact that the principals always rang the bell to tell the staff if there should be outside or inside recess.

I posed the question, "Am I the best person to determine that? What if I am in a conference, in a classroom, or out of the building at a principal's meeting?" Everyone nodded in agreement that that might pose a problem. They talked at their tables for a few minutes then, after awhile, one group proposed that the teacher who was on playground duty for that day and the paraprofessional assigned to playground duty would make the determination if the weather was too inclement to go outside. If so, the paraprofessional would ring the bell to let everyone know. That system worked extremely well, making those responsible for playground duty accountable for the notification.

My Journal Story

_____

_____

_____

_____

_____

_____

_____

_____

_____

_____

_____

_____

_____

_____

_____

_____

_____

_____

Lessons Learned

- It is important to challenge the assumption that it is the right thing to do because "it has always been done that way."

- People will rise to the occasion if given a chance to be thoughtful about a given situation.

- The principal can elicit input about decisions from those impacted by the decisions.

- More heads are more thoughtful about a situation than one head.

Mini Coaching

- When have you been confronted with a situation where people say, "It's always been done that way?"

- What situations do you want to change?

- What are possible ways to confront a situation that you want to change?

- What are some other ways you can think of to involve your staff in decisions that affect them?

Kids Agreeing on What Happened

I ask them to sit on special "problem-solving chairs" in the office and talk about what happened until they are both satisfied that they have one true story.

—Diana Williams

Often when students come to the principal's office, they are both busy telling me what the other one did, pointing the finger at the other person. When tempers are inflamed and the students cannot tell the story because they are so committed to the other one being wrong, I handle it in one of two ways.

If they do not seem angry enough to pose harm to each other, I ask them to sit on special "problem-solving chairs" in the office and talk about what happened until they are both satisfied that they have one true story.

If tempers are such that I think they might be too angry to talk with each other, I put them in separate areas and ask them to write their individual versions of the story. If they are very young children and do not write, I ask them to draw pictures of their version of what happened. Once each has written, I find that it calms them, and then I ask them to read each other's stories and come up with one story to tell me about what happened.

Usually, after some time, they are both able to acknowledge what each of their roles had been in the ruckus. Often, they will say, "He did _____, and I did _____, but we are friends again." Once I determine that they both agree, that each perceives the story the same way, and that they have committed to this being the end of the problem, I ask them to sign off on their own written pieces or the discipline-referral sheet that has been sent to the office, and I send them on their way. I file the documents for future reference in the event that there is another problem or that parents want to know about the problem. These informal forms written by the students are additional documentation to use with parents who might think the school was being unfair with their child. The forms also are used to share with teachers who would want a report of the outcomes with their students.

My Journal Story

Lessons Learned

- Students learn the art of mediating conflict when required to talk it out.

- This process teaches students to assume responsibility for their part of the problem.

- Students learn that there is more than one side to a problem.

- Students are learning to monitor their own discipline.

- We maintained an effective "due process" procedure for students. They had many opportunities for successful behavior.

- I, as principal, was able to gain unique insights into my students with this special interaction.

MC
Mini Coaching

- What is your goal for student discipline?

- What are successful strategies you have used to improve student behavior?

- What ways do you have for students to think about their own roles in a problem?

- As you consider "best practices" for student discipline, what strategies are you using to achieve your goal?

- How do you involve parents in the discipline plan for their children?

The Kids Can't Do Math

You have to stand outside the box to see how the box can be re-designed.

—Charles Handy, Author

The staff was dissatisfied with the progress that many of our students were making, and they were complaining about the lack of assistance of home. It was felt that the students needed an extension to their school day. As usual, the age-old question emerged, "Where was the help coming from and who was going to provide it?" After grappling with the question for a while, the answer appeared suddenly out of nowhere: The teachers would need to devise and implement a plan to provide the extra help because there was no money earmarked for after-school tutoring, and there were no volunteers. A committee of teachers established the tutoring schedule that was based on teacher availability, identified which grade levels would receive help, and the prerequisites for attending the after-school sessions—classroom teachers would need to provide work for the students to practice. My job was to notify parents of the opportunity, establish pick-up methods for the students because there would be no crossing guards or transportation available later in the day (students who rode the bus also attended our school), and obtain permission slips for the students to attend the program. The program started as scheduled, and many of our students did take advantage of the opportunity. The students who received the extra help did benefit from the experience, and the staff had the opportunity to witness those improvements as the school year unfolded, which was rewarding.

My Journal Story

_____

_____

_____

_____

_____

_____

_____

_____

_____

_____

_____

_____

_____

_____

_____

_____

_____

_____

Lessons Learned

- People will solve their own problems if they are allowed that opportunity.

- A school staff can be very innovative when forced to create ways to meet the demands of their students.

- Teachers are concerned about helping the students to achieve.

Mini Coaching

- What ways have you created learning extensions for your students?

- In what ways do you provide for safety measures in after-school learning extensions?

- What type of encouragement will you provide for those teachers who are going the extra mile for their own students as well as others?

Professional-Development Snippet

Maximizing Time for Professional Development With Staff

Time with your staff for planning is one of the most evasive tools a principal can find. There always seems to be a plethora of agenda items and information we must convey to staff members. Often, staff members do not have the time to convey important information to each other. It is difficult to carve out time for professional dialogue. Usually, we are allocated one or two periods of time per month for staff meetings. As we feel compelled to get everything in these narrow windows of time, we lecture for our 45 minutes to an hour on all of the important things we think we are compelled to tell them. Staff members often report that, "Those meetings are a waste of time." Their inattention and glassy-eyed looks at the end of the day tell the story. How do we then convey information to staff with some sparkle? Some ways to maximize time for communication with staff are as follows.

- Communicate by e-mail or in-house newsletters the "administrivia" that staff members need to have.
- Announcements, deadlines, and updates on various issues that require routine information can be provided in writing in multiple media.
- A posted bulletin in a centralized location, an e-mail, a newsletter in everyone's mailbox, text updates, and audio updates are all ways that can be utilized to get routine messages out.

- Staff-meeting times can be used as the time for the staff to help form the agenda with information they would like to share.
- In-house cable networking can be used for intraschool communications as well as for getting the word out to the community.
- Do not be afraid to let go and let staff members co-create the meeting agendas. We had an agenda box where staff members could add agenda items prior to the meeting. They also indicated how much time they would need for their item.

What then do you do with the staff-meeting time? This time can be used for designing and planning actions by the staff in areas that have been determined to be priorities. As student discipline is always at the forefront of the needs of a school, the following is an example of how staff can come together and plan and design actions within the framework and time limits of a staff meeting. The purpose of the meeting should be given to staff ahead of time, so they can reflect upon the topic prior to the meeting. How often do we attend meetings for which there is no noticeable purpose except in the mind of the planner? A notification might look like the following.

"Dear Staff,

The purpose of this week's staff meeting is to improve our overall, schoolwide discipline plan. Please bring your ideas, and be prepared to collaborate around this important topic."

Then, for instance, on the meeting day, divide the staff into task groups at tables to discuss the following areas:

- **Prioritizing transitional areas in the school needing attention.** Assuming that individual teachers have a pretty good command of student discipline, the problems usually occur at transitional times where there is less one-on-one supervision, such as playgrounds, hallways, bathrooms, between classes, lunchtime, recess time, before school, after school, and on buses.
- **Identify the top 20% repeat offenders in the school.** Often, it is 20% of the student population that is giving you 80% of the grief. The 20% makes it feel like the whole school is out of control. Identifying the problem students enables the staff to make an intentional plan for these students.
- **Identify resources for these children.** Possible resources include staff advocates for each child, volunteers, special behavior plans, intense academic interventions, counselors, and resource coaches.
- **Identify resources for individual teachers needing assistance.** Counselors, coaches, a partner teacher, the principal, a volunteer, a professional-development program addressing classroom procedures or management or discipline issues are possibilities. Read books on discipline approaches. Videotape yourself teaching, and either with or without a trusted but critical friend, critique.

Have each group report their findings to the whole group. Ask for a volunteer committee to draft the plan and report back at the next staff meeting. As this process will take about one hour, the work will be ongoing. Once the committee reports back, assign tasks to be carried out, and develop a timeline for each action. Commit the plan to writing. Review assignments and special tasks on the part of the staff to make sure it happens. Check back after the plan has been in effect for a while. Monitor and celebrate successes!

Dear Principal,

As the grandmother of one of your students, I want to express my gratitude to you for the part you have played in turning around the life of a frustrated child. I was so proud to see him receive his honor roll award yesterday. He had been diagnosed in his early school years as "developmentally disabled" and look at him now! This little guy is on his way now. All I can say is Thank you, thank you, thank you!!!! You have made a difference!

Mrs. Richardson

CHAPTER

A school administrator is an educational leader who promotes the success of all students by collaborating with families and community members, responding to diverse community interests and needs, and mobilizing community resources.

LEADING A DIVERSE FAMILY AND COMMUNITY CONNECTION

INTRODUCTION
Strong Parents + Strong Communities = Strong Partnerships

Throughout the year, we looked for opportunities to invite families into the school setting and to foster two-way communication between home and school. Often, schools communicate with parents in a one-way direction, by informing them what they want from parents. Less often, they provide two-way communication opportunities, asking parents what they want from the school. Our way of asking parents for input consisted of opportunities to take surveys, to offer input in our newsletters, to make appointments to come in and talk with various staff members about identified topics, and to participate in frequent "coffee and donuts with the principal" conversations. Parents were included on our school-improvement committee, and professional-development opportunities were developed and encouraged by and for parents. When school was dismissed for professional development for the staff, we informed the parents about the nature of the professional development and how it was making our school better. We took pains to make sure they knew that we were continuing our learning to better our work on behalf of their children. We adopted the tag line, "We are a community of leaders and learners!"

We planned activities where parents learned with their children. In addition to various curriculum nights where parents made and received learning materials to use with their children at home, we organized a parent-run resource room where parents could get learning assistance and information

from staff as well as from other nurturing parents. The teachers assumed responsibility for partnering with parents to cochair various parent activities. They signed up for various parent committees and activities at the annual retreat planning. (See Chapter 2.)

We applied for and received several grants, including a grant to implement a technology program; a venture capital grant from our state Department of Education; a U.S. Department of Education National Science Foundation Grant; and various small grants specific to the community, such as the local Center of Science and Industry grant and the Ohio Department of Agriculture grant. Active parents provided invaluable technical support and expertise for many of these grants. We didn't know what talent we had in the community until we reached out. In addition, we received a grant to fund a part-time parent-involvement specialist who was hired from the community. She, along with the parent organization, was active in soliciting local businesses for donations and services for our students. Parents not only became instrumental in serving on our grant committees, they became familiar with the curriculum and the testing procedures through programs held at the school. We forged opportunities for parents to offer comments and suggestions and to serve as partners in making our school a great community school. We prided ourselves on being a "community of leaders and learners."

Celebratory Notes for Doing Good Things

Building relationships is the key to effective parent involvement.

—Diana Williams

One day, a fifth-grade student intervened between two classmates who were getting ready to fight on the playground. Rather than getting in the mix himself, he parted them and talked them down before an approaching teacher could get to the ruckus. The teacher brought them all into the office and told me how Terrell had stopped the fight. I commended him and concluded the proceedings. I was so impressed that I took the opportunity to send an "I was a leader today" note home to his parents. I had never seen his parents, but at the next opportunity for parents to come to school for an activity, they attended and made a point of telling me that they were Terrell's parents. They were just beaming. We celebrated his leadership once again, and they continued on with the evening's events. I noticed that they always attended programs and meetings from that time on.

My Journal Story

Lessons Learned

- I did not realize the power a principal's affirmation had on a parent's perception of the school.

- Little things, like positive notes that don't cost a lot of money, go a long way in eliciting parent participation.

- Building relationships is the key to effective parent involvement.

- Positive two-way communication between parents and school personnel demonstrates to students that parents and school personnel are on the same team. This sets the tone for fostering respect for schooling from the student.

Mini Coaching

- How do you acknowledge the good things your students do? How do you communicate those positive things to parents?

- How does your staff acknowledge the positive things that occur with the parents?

- What would you like a positive-acknowledgment program to look like?

Getting the Support of Unruly Parents

Parents give us their best children. It is up to us to work with them and not give up.

—Diana Williams

One day when I was an assistant principal, the teacher in charge of discipline came looking for me. Her eyes were large and her face was pale as she informed me that a mother was there who was very, very angry, and she was afraid. I went fearlessly with her, yet later I reflected on what could I have done to protect either her or myself. At any rate, I met the mother with her. She ranted and raved about how this teacher had unfairly put her child into time out. I listened. When her wrath had disappeared somewhat, I calmly asserted that I knew this teacher to be a very fair one. It was a stroke of special wisdom that comes at a moment of grace when I said, "We try to offer students the consequences that will make them self-reliant so that, when they get out into the workplace, they will be able to monitor themselves and will be able to keep good jobs." Those were the magic words. She turned to her daughter and said, "They are right. That's why I can't keep a job—because I have a temper. Honey, I want better for you! They are telling you right." The rest of the conference was making a plan for improved behavior on the part of the student.

My Journal Story

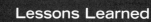

Lessons Learned

- I believe all parents want a better life for their children. They may not always be able to express it in a way that is acceptable to us, but once we can work with them to identify that we all want the same thing, we have a shot at forging a strong parent bond with the school.

- Sometimes, it is important just to listen—not to defend or become defensive, but to just listen even as a parent vents anger.

- Parents give us their best children. It is up to us to work with them and not give up.

- It is important that the students view us as being on the same page with their parents.

Mini Coaching

- Think of a time you have had a great relationship with a parent. What made that relationship great?

- Think of a difficult parent situation. How can you use what you know from the positive relationship to foster a better relationship with the difficult parent?

Williams, D. (2008). "Getting the Support of Unruly Parents" originally appeared in the *Principals Office*, an ezine for school administrators from The Ohio State University's P–12 Project and Interprofessional Commission. The *Principal's Office* is available at www.principalsoffice.osu.edu.

It's a Smelly Situation

Tact is the art of putting your foot down without stepping on anyone's toes.

—Lawrence J. Peter, Educator and Author

The road between an adversarial and an advocatory relationship is strewn with all types of roadblocks and opportunities. This aptly characterized the association of Mrs. Jelloby with our school. She was a strong personality who intimidated the staff with her directness and request for help (the help part was questionable, unless you focused on the message as oppose to the messenger). She had two sons in our school who experienced a great deal of academic challenge. The older son was two years below his grade level, and the younger son was experiencing some obvious learning difficulties; he was repeating first grade and not having a lot of academic success. The first-grade teacher shared her concerns with Mrs. Jelloby, but Mrs. Jelloby refused to permit her son to be evaluated by the school psychologist. She had difficulty understanding what the teacher was saying and felt the school was not providing an adequate education for either of her boys. The teacher, because of the parent's mannerisms, felt threatened and asked me to remove her permanently from the building. I disagreed with this course of action and decided to take a different approach. Mrs. Jelloby always brought her children to school and remained with them until the bell rang and they entered the building. I started to really notice her as an individual and not just as a parent dropping off a child. I discovered she usually had a scowl on her face that suggested the message, "Keep your distance." No one in my school tells me to keep my distance, so I made it my business to have conversation with her every morning. At first, it was only a casual good morning greeting—even the rudest person will respond to a nice friendly gesture that says I'm glad you are here. As I began to initiate more conversation with her, I uncovered her concerns and fears. She felt that she and her children were not respected. After developing a relationship with her, I arranged a conference with the first-grade teacher, and we sat down to discuss Timothy's problems. Within a couple of months, Mrs. Jelloby had agreed to have Timmy evaluated, and, as a consequence, he received services for his identified learning disabilities. In the meantime, I suggested that she volunteer during the breakfast program; and later on, when a vacancy occurred, I hired her as a crossing guard. She did her job well because she loved the students and was interested in helping them to be safe. She had the capacity to express the same love for other students that she felt for her own children.

There's a saying, "When the going is too easy, check and make sure you're not going downhill." Some of the staff members began to complain about her body odor. I must admit, I had noticed it also, but was hoping that it would go away. Like most things left not addressed, it didn't. When I knew teachers were complaining indirectly, it was a red flag saying they would be coming directly to me with the same complaint. Guess what, they did! At that moment, I wished someone else could have been the principal. I could not find a volunteer, so I listened with a wise ear and committed to resolving the issue. The question was how was this to happen? Mustering up most of the skills and courage that I possessed, I called Mrs. Jelloby into the office and after she was seated I said, "You know, I care a lot about you, and therefore I need to tell you something that is very personal, but it needs to be said. You have a body odor that is offensive to others, and we need to explore ways to eliminate it." She started to cry. I must admit I was totally blown away by that experience. She explained how she always kept the boys clean and used the detergent she had to wash their clothes. I commended her on how well her children looked, but I reminded her that she could not neglect herself. We discussed regular routines that could be used without impacting a lot on what was available to maintain her children's hygiene. She left my office shortly before noon and returned about two o'clock the same day. She smelled as sweet as a freshly picked rose. She continued to volunteer at the school and became one of my strongest supporters. Upon leaving the school, I continued to hear from her until she passed away, 15 years after that incident in my office.

My Journal Story

Lessons Learned

- Sometimes things are not what they seem to be. The school and I would have lost one of our dearest friends if I had not taken the time to reach out to a woman that was hurting on the inside while maintaining a strong façade.

- Heroes and heroines are sometimes just the people around you who perform heroic deeds when the need arises—I failed to mention that Mrs. Jelloby was hit in the leg with a BB pellet while performing her duties as a crossing guard. Did she resign from the job after the incident? No, she did not, because she felt the students really needed her to be on that corner.

- When people share their personal stories, it helps you to gain a better understanding of individuals and their needs.

Mini Coaching

- Can you think of a time when the staff placed you in an uncomfortable situation and how you responded to the challenge?

- When interpersonal relations among the adults appeared to be tense, what are some things you did to restore the positive climate?

- What are the indicators that signal when parents are willing to trust the school's assessment of their child's needs?

- What skills have you used when engaged in potentially explosive conversations with adults?

Treasures in Trash

The manner of giving is worth more than the gift.

—Pierre Corneille, French Dramatist

Having a school partner in the community can be a very positive asset to any school. The partner or school adopter can provide the school with valuable resources, people, as well as financial assistance. Adopters, which refer to businesses, agencies, and/or organizations, have various reasons for adopting schools. Many businesses and organizations that become involved with schools feel they can genuinely make a difference in the overall educational process. Others have good intentions but have failed to evaluate their resources that can be made available to the school, which results in an adoption on paper without any real substance. Some become involved because the business is placed in a position to gain recognition within the community. Hopefully, our school was adopted because our adopter wanted to make a difference in the lives of the boys and girls that attended our school.

Once the formalities associated with adoption were completed, the business and the school established a line of communication that would be used to facilitate the relationship. I was especially pleased to be adopted by a large organization. However, a specific department or division was identified to become the adopting segment of the company. This department had limited resources that resulted in some of its employees volunteering to tutor at the school during their lunch hour. The identified students were not excited about the possibility of having an interrupted noon recess. Some of the employees set up a Christmas hat-and-glove tree that was used to collect hats and gloves for the students. The collected items were given to the students prior to winter break. One young couple chose to donate money to the tree project in lieu of exchanging gifts with each other. The people within the department appeared to take the adoption very seriously, as evidenced by their efforts to identify activities that would contribute in a meaningful way to the education and welfare of the students.

One day, I received a call from the corporate office of the business. They called to inform me about the supplies and equipment that were available to the school as a result of the renovations that were occurring within their offices. I agreed to accept the items, thinking or dreaming that we would be getting a lot of useful materials, maybe some decent office furniture. What we received consisted of outdated computer equipment that was incompatible with the school's computers and our computer programs, an assortment of paper products, and a high-intensity surgical lamp. Of the items received, the lamp was the most significant because it could be used in our health clinic. We kept those things that were useful and trashed the rest, including the computers. We acknowledged the thoughtful gifts.

The treasure existed within the relationship that was established between the school and its adopter. This was an evolving process. After the give away and our gracious acceptance of the gifts, the business seemed more interested in increasing its activity with the school. The auditorium in their building was made available for our use during the school's end of the year programs; they even provided the refreshments. They sponsored several campaigns that used the school's site to develop an awareness of health-related issues within the school's community, and they provided speakers for our career-day programs. We had to learn to tailor our needs to the resources that were made available by our adopter. What did the school do for the business? We made greeting cards that could be distributed within the hospital complex, our choir sang Christmas carols around the facility during the holiday season, and we provided students to participate in their disaster drills.

My Journal Story

Lessons Learned

- We need to be grateful for the gifts that are offered.

- Sometimes, we are tested to determine if we are endowed with the wisdom and humbleness to accept those things that may not be what we desire, but yet may have a greater significance down the road.

- Once a gift is received, it's up to the receiver to determine how it is used.

Mini Coaching

- If you could wave a magic wand, what resources would you want from a school-community partnership?

- What plan do you have for building this partnership?

- How do you envision the partnership meeting the needs of your students?

Deep Dialogue Around Cultural Conflict

I believe we can change the world if we start listening to one another again. Simple, honest, human conversation. Not mediation, negotiation, problem-solving, debate, or public meetings. Simple, truthful conversation where we each have a chance to speak, we each feel heard, and we each listen well.

—Margaret Wheatley, Author

One day, there were loud voices in the hallway as teachers returned from dismissing the children from the playground to go home. It turned out to be several of the teachers who had witnessed an altercation between one of the white teachers and an African-American mother picking her child up in the car. The teacher had been trying to contact the parent to discuss the progress of the child. When the teacher approached the parent and started asking her why she had not returned notes and calls, the parent admonished her not to talk to her in "that tone." The teacher, who had a loud voice and was an assertive type herself, shook her finger at the parent and assured her she wasn't using a hostile tone. One thing led to another, until one of the African-American teachers intervened, told the parent that the teacher in question meant no harm, and smoothed over the situation. The two teachers were friends, so as they were walking to the office the white teacher felt comfortable in asking her black friend if she had been out of line. They were quickly involved in intense dialogue about the situation. Several other staff members had been drawn into the conversation. By the time the group arrived in my office, everyone was weighing in on what had happened. The conversation had become so intense and animated that I invited the half dozen teachers to sit down around the conference table so we could continue the dialogue.

The conversation covered issues like nuances of how white teachers approach black parents. In the situation in question, some felt that the pointing of the finger at the parent was accusatory and showed a lack of respect. The teacher felt that she was making a point. Some of the black teachers felt that some of the white teachers did not respect the black parents. Some of the teachers felt that for the most part, black parents did not care about the education of their children, as evidenced by them not returning phone calls and notes.

There was a very honest airing of feelings about racial attitudes that day. One incident unleashed a wide range of tensions that had been resting just beneath the surface. I'm reminded of a book entitled *It's the Little Things* by Lena Williams (2000). Her premise is that there are racial insensitivities that occur to which we have either become desensitized or that blow up in our faces. This sticky issue that developed at school reminded me that it is important to look beneath the surface and have opportunities to have deep conversation in order to gain understanding. In the words of Margaret Wheatley (2002), in *Turning to One Another,*

Human conversation is the most ancient and easiest way to cultivate the conditions for change—personal change, community and organizational change, planetary change. If we can sit together and talk about what's important to us, we begin to come alive. We share what we see, what we feel, and we listen to what others see and feel. (p. 3)

My Journal Story

_____

_____

_____

_____

_____

_____

_____

_____

_____

_____

_____

_____

_____

_____

_____

_____

_____

_____

Lessons Learned

- Sometimes, the only solution to a problem is heartfelt conversation.

- Sensitive topics such as race are best discussed in a climate of trust. It is no small task to foster a climate of trust among staff members.

- Often, it is helpful to get the perspective of a trusted colleague when in doubt about one's own behavior.

- It is important to understand another's perspective, without judging, before a problem can be solved.

Mini Coaching

- When have you had to mediate a disagreement between staff members or between staff and parents?

- What tools did you draw upon to mediate understandings?

- What situations that are just below the surface threaten to blow up if not addressed?

- In what ways could you address the problem? Think of an additional way. Think of three more ideas.

Williams, D. (2008). "Deep Dialogue Around Cultural Conflict" originally appeared in the *Principals Office,* an ezine for school administrators from The Ohio State University's P–12 Project and Interprofessional Commission. The *Principal's Office* is available at www.principalsoffice.osu.edu.

Planning for Parent Conferences
Student-Led Conferencing

We are a community of leaders and learners.

—Diana Williams

One of the best ways for students to accept responsibility for their learning is for them to have to explain their learning to someone else. For the second round of parent conferences, several of our classrooms planned the following format for the evening.

The parents or a family representative arrived in the classroom with their child. The student and parents visited the desk of the student where a portfolio of work had been prepared. The portfolio included (1) work that the student was proud of, (2) work that the student felt could have been better, (3) any infraction notes, (4) any positive acknowledgements, such as stickers or "caught you being good" notes, and (5) information about the class, such as schedules, special projects, and classroom newsletters. The job of the students was to walk their parents through their portfolios and to conference with their parents. Some preplanned and prerehearsed talking points for the students, in addition to explaining the portfolios to the parents, were (1) What did I do well? (2) What could I have done better? and (3) What goals do I have for the rest of the year?

Once the parents heard the reports, the student introduced their parents to the teacher. Time was then arranged for further discussion with the teacher on specific questions or interventions. The teacher also had a generic portfolio ready to hand parents with tips for helping their children.

The staff planned for children who could not bring a parent to conference night by scheduling a meeting with the principal or another adult advocate to go over their portfolio and to make new goals.

My Journal Story

_____

_____

_____

_____

_____

_____

_____

_____

_____

_____

_____

_____

_____

_____

_____

_____

_____

_____

_____

Lessons Learned

- This format for parent conferences made the students accountable for their own reports.

- Student-led conferencing developed leadership and responsibility in students for their own learning. This supported our school vision that "We are a community of leaders and learners."

- The parents reported that they got a lot more information from their children about what was going on in school through this format.

- Teachers gained greater appreciation for the parents as they witnessed them interacting with their children and taking an active role in the conference.

- The teachers who developed this process took ownership for it and insured its success.

Mini Coaching

- When have staff members brought innovative ideas to you that they wanted to try?

- What was your response to the innovation and to the teachers?

- What are some ways you can foster risk taking among your staff members?

- How can you support teacher innovation?

- What are some other ways parent conferencing can be more successful?

Moving Day

In any given set of circumstances, the proper course of action is determined by subsequent events.

—McDonald's Corollary to Murphy's Law

Overcrowded conditions within the school created the need to seek classroom space away from the school site. Student numbers had to be decreased because they were in violation of the teachers' union contract. All available space in the building was used to capacity. The central-office administrators suggested several schools across town that could be used to house our students. The parents were adamantly opposed to the possibility of having their children bussed that far away— approximately five miles—and they became quite vocal. The minister at the church located a half-block from the school became aware of our dilemma and offered to allow the school to use two classrooms that were located in a wing of the church. Before accepting the offer, various department supervisors had to inspect the property to determine whether it met the standards that were necessary to house our students. The facilities at the church did meet the prescribed standards, the minister's offer was accepted, and the process of reorganization began.

Preparations that included staff involvement were undertaken to identify which grade level was going to move, hire the additional teaching staff, organize the school schedule to accommodate the off-campus students' needs, order the additional school supplies and materials, and keep parents of the affected students as well as the school community informed about the need for reorganization and progress toward that goal. All the above occurred in a timely manner, and the big day arrived.

There was one situation that I had not anticipated and that was the abundance of people—central-office staff, parents, news reporter, and the naturally curious. The noise outside the building reached a festive pitch. Television and newspaper reporters were interviewing parents and students as they entered the school grounds; and of course, all the students wanted to be on TV. When the bells rang for the start of the school day, the excitement dissipated, and the teachers brought their classes into the building. The parents and news media followed, and each wanted to have a discussion with me. It seemed to be a sea of movement both inside the building and outside. I had to make a decision as to how this rather chaotic situation was going to be handled. The decision was easy. The hour for the march down the street was drawing near and I needed to move the first graders to their new home. So, I invited the parents to go to the library and wait for my return, and the news-media personnel were given a similar option to wait in another designated place. The parents did go to the library as directed, the news media moved away from me, and the staff and I were able to execute our plan. Without a hitch, the students were gathered, and we paraded down the street to our "new" school home. Later, one of the reporters asked how we were able to move so smoothly. He had followed us to the church and was very impressed with the appearance of the classrooms, the serenity of the students, and the preparation of the teachers. He described the situation as appearing like a normal school day. What did the news media expect?

My Journal Story

- It's wise to be receptive to people and community resources that are beyond the walls of the school.

- Extraordinary planning and preparations must occur in order to resolve extraordinary situations.

- Learn to anticipate the unexpected and to stay focused on the task at hand when challenges occur, while addressing the needs of the immediate situation. It's easy to become sidetracked when the unexpected happens.

Mini Coaching

- When faced with challenging situations that require change, what do you see yourself doing to drive the change?

- As you plan for change, how willing are you to involve others?

- If change requires support outside of your immediate resources, what will you do first? Next? What else?

Mom on the Run

There are many survival needs of students that surpass the immediacy of schoolwork.

—Diana Williams

I remember one intervention assistance team (IAT) meeting where we were considering what to do with a student who had arrived at our school in the middle of the week, in the middle of the school year, with no supplies, not much documentation, and with no spark of life in his eyes. He soon proved to be behind in his grade level, uninterested, and unmotivated. He was quickly referred to the team to see what could be done.

Our process was to invite all interested parties, including the parent, to the IAT meeting. Although we shared the school social worker with several other schools, she was a part of our IAT meetings as often as possible. As there was some question as to the legitimate address verification, the social worker attended this meeting.

The mother came to the meeting, and after listening quietly to all of the "educationalese" about her son's lack of progress, she very quietly told us that she and her son were living out of the local women's shelter. She told us how they had had to flee in the middle of the night from an abusive boyfriend, taking not much more than their pajamas. She was trying to do the best that she could.

The school social worker stepped up to the plate and asked if she could meet with the mother and child. We agreed to table the educational-intervention conversation until the next time. The social worker took the mother and son to her favorite social agencies to get much-needed assistance for them. The assistance included finding some clothing, including a winter coat, for the boy.

The student came back to school better dressed and a little more trusting of our school. Unfortunately, when their housing came through, they moved on to another location. I often think about that student and his mother. I was so appreciative of the school social worker that day and how it really does "take a village to raise a child."

My Journal Story

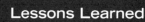

Lessons Learned

- Initially, I was annoyed that we had to accommodate a student whose parent seemingly was irresponsible. We were concerned that this would be one more student with low-testing success to impact our school achievement scores.

- I learned that there are many survival needs of students that surpass the immediacy of schoolwork.

- I came to admire the resilience of this mother and child.

- I admired even more the role that professionals, such as social workers, play in the care of the total child.

Mini Coaching

- What structures do you have in place to help you catch the students with severe social, emotional, or behavioral problems?

- What other interventions would you like to implement?

- How will you work with your staff to meet the needs of the total child?

- How will you bring parents to the table to help their children?

- What other resources do you need, and how will you get them?

What Kind of Doctor Are You Anyway?

You cannot please everyone all of the time.

—Diana Williams

Our district had a policy of excluding students who had head lice. This procedure was administered and monitored by the school nurse. Each time the nurse issued an exclusion letter, she would give me a copy, so I would be aware of students who needed a "healthy head" clearance before returning to school.

On one particular day, a mother returned to school the day after she had received an exclusion letter. She stated that she had cleansed her child's head of lice the night before and demanded that her child be cleared to stay in school. Since the nurse was not in that day, I agreed to check the child's head with the explanation that only if I saw nothing suspicious the child would be allowed to stay. If I saw any suspicious evidence of nits, she would have to come back when the nurse was present. The student's mother protested, "She had done everything she was told to do."

I took the customary wooden stick and began to look for nits. I saw what I thought to be nits and pointed them out to the mother. Annoyed, she said, "Oh, that's just dandruff!" I looked some more and saw more evidence of nits. I told her I was sorry, but she would have to work some more on them and return tomorrow. She grabbed up her daughter and heatedly left the office with the parting admonition, "What kind of doctor are you anyway?"

My Journal Story

Lessons Learned

- A PhD does not necessarily mean you will have the tools to help in every situation!

- You cannot please everyone all of the time.

- Some situations you just have to let go and laugh about!

- This was a sobering and humbling experience.

- I thought I would like to rethink the exclusion policy for head lice.

Mini Coaching

- Think of a time you have been humbled as a professional. How did you handle the situation?

- What policies are troublesome for you that you would like to rethink?

- What situations were you able to step back from and laugh about?

- How do you let go of unresolved situations?

Bring Your Drugs to School

When the spirit of people is strong, focused, and vibrant, wonderful things happen.

—Harrison Owen, Author, Photographer, and Consultant

Our adopt-a-school partner wanted to do a project with the school that would have a community outreach. Because the partnership was with a medical facility, the corporation had a strong desire to improve the health of our families by providing good information that people could use when making health-related decisions. In one of the meetings, it was decided that our health-education initiative would be started with a call for outdated prescription drugs; it was assumed that most people have outdated prescription medications sitting around the house or in the medicine cabinet. Information about the collection was sent home—it was to be collected on a specific date and time. Medications were to be brought to school by adults; they could not be sent with the students.

The person bringing in the oldest prescription would receive $50.00.

The collection was held at our school in the library, which was located in the lower level of the building. The partner wanted the activity to happen at the school so that people would be aware of the joint effort to focus on family as well as children. Information on health issues was made available, and medical people were on site to answer health-related questions. The drug collection was highly successful; several medium-sized boxes were filled with outdated drugs. The oldest bottle of prescription drugs collected was 52 years old. The adopt-a-school partner was pleased with the level of participation by our school's parents and the amount of outdated drugs that was collected.

My Journal Story

Lessons Learned

- Parents will participate in activities other than those that have their children involved.

- Parents who participated in the drug collection seemed pleased and expressed a willingness to become involved in another such activity.

- Having the activity at the building did send a message that the school was interested in the welfare of the family and community.

Mini Coaching

- How do you respond when a community partner or some other school-board-approved agency makes a proposal for involving your school in an activity?

- From your review of data about school-sponsored community-outreach programs, what inferences do you draw from the information?

- How would you determine the activities that would be most beneficial for your school community, and who would be involved?

- What are the possibilities for programs such as this in the school and how would it affect the school's image?

- Where will you go from here? When will you do that?

Professional-Development Snippet

Building Parent and Community Partnerships

I recently overheard a mother talking about her son's school while I was sitting in a waiting room of a doctor's office. She was telling her confidante that her son's teacher had sent a three-page form home to be filled out the same night he sent it home. She had just had a new baby, and the grandmother had delivered the form from the school to the mom. The mother wondered out loud why the form had not been sent prior to the deadline or why at least she had not been given a weekend to work on it. This illustrates how little things can upset parents and breach their cooperation with the school. With a slight adjustment on the part of the school, these issues can often be eliminated.

Use comments from parents to produce a professional dialogue with staff about how to foster two-way (home to school and school to home) communication as opposed to one-way (school to home) communication. The following process is one way a school can foster better communication with the home:

> Step 1. Invite parents to a coffee klatch with the principal. Host a donuts-and-coffee morning every Friday in selected months as parents drop off their children. When they come in, hand them a slip of paper that says, "If I could make one change at school, it would be _____."

> Step 2. At a staff meeting, pass out a few of the comment sheets to each grouping of four to five staff members. Ask them to discuss the comments and develop strategies to accommodate the requests where possible. Ask them to be creative and to think out of the box.

> Step 3. Prioritize the concerns, and develop a plan for action for selected strategies.

> Step 4. Let parents know that you are taking their concerns seriously. Select a few to run in the newsletter, and invite discussion about what to do about the issues. A further extension is to take the ideas to a school-reform committee composed of staff and parent leaders to work on the issues.

It's a good idea for both a teacher and a parent leader to co-chair an event. Following are several ideas for involving parents in their children's learning.

Family Concert Picnic With a Local Band

There was a popular local musician who donated his time and music at a nominal cost. The band arrived at lunchtime. We asked parents to bring picnic baskets and blankets, and we all ate on the school grounds, listening to the wonderful sounds of the band. This was a very successful end-of-the-year program, but it could also be a great kick-off-the-year activity as well.

Center of Science and Industry School

We partnered with our local Center of Science and Industry (COSI) to do COSI school. The staff spent several hours of professional development with the science-center staff learning how to be docents for the various exhibits. The science-center staff had aligned the professional development and various student exhibits with our curriculum. On science day, we closed the school, and everyone—including parents, custodians, and the secretary—loaded buses, and we all went off to school for the day at the science center. Students, staff, and parents rotated through the preplanned interactive exhibits all day long. The principal was "the wizard" for an introductory activity using fire and noise. This required a lot of preplanning and organization between the school staff and the science staff, but the day was well worth it. We had a large parent participation rate as all parents were invited and had ample time to request time off from work to join us for the day.

Math Night

This night, we invited parents in to rotate through stations with their children and use all kinds of math manipulatives and math games to teach concepts. There was a food rotation where everyone ate as well.

Reading Night

Reading night was similar to math night except the activities were geared around how parents can help their child read at home. Parents and students rotated through the various reading stations with various activities. Books were given away as door prizes, and food was again one of the rotations!

Science Night

Science night was really hyped, as we had the astronomy lab planetarium for the evening, funded by the National Science Foundation. This was a room-sized, darkened dome with the solar system projected onto the ceiling. Parents and students had to crouch down and go through an attached tunnel to enter the planetarium. There were lines of parents waiting their turn to enter the dome with their children. We had other science rotations as well, and again, we had a food rotation!

Field Day

Many schools have field days. We had the usual field day, but we invited parents to participate as well.

Talent Show

This was a highlight of the year. Many schools have talent shows at the end of the year. Each classroom prescreened and selected one act. The highlight was the act that the adult staff prepared each year to surprise the students. One year, it was a hip-hop act with the principal and teachers dancing and singing to the lyrics, "School's Out!" The sight of the staff in jeans and turned-around ball caps brought the house down!

Staff-Student Volleyball Game

This became a beloved yearly activity. Parents came with their chairs to watch and cheer on their teams.

Spaghetti Supper for Curriculum Night

We hosted several nights to explain testing requirements to parents. We combined these informational meetings with a spaghetti dinner!

Honors Assemblies for Each Grading Period

Most schools have recognition events. We extended the honors to celebrate as many students as possible.

First Day of School Conference-Night Coffee and Donuts With the Principal

I took the opportunity to invite parents to talk with me about their concerns, issues, and suggestions as often as possible. These opportunities included having donuts and coffee in the library or in my office.

Phone Calls Home and Positive Notes Home

On one occasion, I wrote a note home about a student who had broken up a fight on the playground. I was so impressed with this young man's actions that I wanted his parents to know what a peacemaker he had been. They became forever loyal and supportive of the school. This encouraged me to write more positive letters home and to make more phone calls when students and staff excelled.

Eaglettes

Three teachers who were involved in drill teams with their own children decided to start a drill team at school. They worked hard to secure costumes and worked with parents on being boosters to this wildly popular activity. The girls were awarded merits and demerits—with the threat of not being able to participate if they accrued too many demerits. When the girls finally started competing, our stands were full of parents even on early Saturday mornings. I jokingly chided parents at one large turnout, yelling to the stands, "I want to see you all at PTA meeting next week!" Unfortunately, a male teacher who had plans to provide an activity for the boys was staff reduced, and we never got a special activity of this scope started for the boys.

Multicultural Fair

Each classroom selected a country to study for a unit. They immersed themselves into the culture of their selected country, into the food, the dress, and the customs. Parents were invited to contribute particularly, as many were of the nationalities selected. We designated one night for the fair. The students stayed after school for pizza and practice with their teachers. Parents came after work at 6:00 p.m. for an evening of cultural immersion as the students danced and sang their acts, as food of the many nations was tasted, and as there was an aura of a peaceful uniting of nations for an evening.

Hiring a Part-Time Community Member to Stimulate Parent Involvement

We used grant money to hire a community person to serve as a parent-involvement specialist. She worked tirelessly to bring parents into the school. It was helpful having an extra pair of hands to nurture the relationships of the parent community.

Technology Workshops

We identified a parent who was prominent in the technical field at a local business. He and his wife were involved parents and offered to volunteer in any way they could. When it came time to write for a large technology grant, we tapped his expertise to sit on our committee and help with the decision making. This partnership lasted for the duration of his child's time in our school. He was a vital part of our technology expansion, training, and innovation.

Trip to Tuskegee Institute and the Space Center

Our parent committee, under the leadership of our parent-involvement specialist, solicited donations from businesses and conducted fundraisers so that the fourth- and fifth-grade students could go on a field trip to the Tuskegee Institute and the Space Center in Huntsville, Alabama. We went on a chartered bus during spring break with both parent and staff volunteers.

Monthly Advisory-Committee Meeting

In addition to our formal parent group, we invited parent representatives from various classrooms to serve on an advisory committee. I invited parents through newsletters to submit their issues to the committee. They were all welcome to come to the meetings as well.

Inclusion of Community Representatives on Grant-Writing Committees

Often, community members can bring another perspective to the process. Also, this provides visibility for your school as one that is progressive and tuned into the community.

End-Of-the-Year-Ceremony Partnership With a Local Junior College

We borrowed beautiful blue cushioned chairs every year from our local community college for our end of the year "Circle of Life" culminating activity. The college delivered and picked up the chairs for us. They added a special formality and beauty to our ceremony, which was held outdoors every year on the last day of school. The chairs were arranged in a large semicircle facing a podium, with the student chairs completing the circle. The fifth graders marched out to the music "The Circle of Life" (John & Rice, 1994) and encircled their parents and families before taking their seats.

Take a Kid to College

Our local university offered a program called "Take a Kid to College." We were awarded a grant to take a busload of students to the university for planned activities, a tour, and a luncheon.

Local University Extension Center (Urban 4H and Garden Club)

Our local extension center made a grant available that enabled our students to plant a community garden. Teacher volunteers who loved to garden and local parents and students tended the garden in the summer months as well.

Community-Services-Information Night

We expanded our open-house night to include a community-services exhibit as well. Parents could pick up brochures and sign up for such services as a library card, parent-support groups, and resources-referral information.

Partnership With Recreation Department

During two years of my tenure at my last school, the local recreation center was undergoing extensive renovation. The center director asked if they could use our gym at night so they could continue their programs. They would provide staffing for basketball and games for the younger children right after school and for the older teens in the evening. This arrangement worked out well, although we had to overcome some turf issues of some staff not wanting to share supplies and space. We came to view the supplies and space as belonging not to us personally but to the taxpayers and parents in our community.

Visit as a Staff to Neighborhood Church at the Beginning of the Year

We were invited, as a staff, to attend a local church at the beginning of the school year. Not everyone went, but several staff members did attend. We were warmly recognized by the congregation as the staff from the neighborhood elementary school.

Local Deli for Teacher-Appreciation Coupons

There was a local deli that the staff often ordered lunch from. We were well known at the deli. When it came time for teacher-appreciation week, I went to the owner and asked if I could pay him to provide a coupon for a free breakfast for each of our staff members. He gave me a very good rate for a full breakfast including tip. I made up the coupon thanking the teachers for their hard work, and he made sure their coupons were honored in a special way during the two-week period. Teachers enjoyed meeting early to have a special breakfast.

Various Larger Department Stores

Our local businesses offered various services and merchandise to our students at various times. These included free eye exams, bicycles for scholars, and honors prizes, as well as food and supplies for our many programs.

Various Charitable Organizations

We maintained a cooperative working relationship with various social-service organizations. We were open to providing space for social workers to meet with parents at the school.

Looking for a Few Good Men

This was our initiative to bring male role models into the school. We sought out fathers, uncles, and grandfathers to become volunteers in the school. The staff also asked husbands and friends to volunteer. We assigned these men to become mentors to identified males in our school. We exercised the usual safeguards of screening by the district volunteer office and by always having students and mentors in proximity of staff.

CHAPTER

Standard Five

A school administrator is an educational leader who promotes the success of all students by acting with integrity, fairness, and in an ethical manner.

THE ETHICS OF LEADERSHIP

If a school administrator is an educational leader who promotes the success of all students by acting with integrity, fairness, and in an ethical manner, then he or she must wear outside armor to reflect those qualities.

—Essie Richardson

INTRODUCTION
Integrity + Fairness = Ethics

You, the principal, are placed in an uncomfortable position because parents are unhappy about a grade assigned to their child and they are demanding that this grade be changed. You have to make a decision as to whether you honor the parents' request or support the teacher's judgment. This becomes an ethical decision. Would it be fair to the school community and other parents if you changed grades based upon the parents' requests? If their request is acknowledged and favorably acted upon, would their moment of favor toward you turn to disdain, mistrust, and lack of respect for you as an authority figure? Would the teacher and other staff members feel that you acted with integrity if you changed grades without their knowledge, input, or consent? Such decisions must be weighed against a set of principals or code of ethics, which drives the way we think and behave. The school leader has the responsibility of maintaining the respect and confidence of the school staff, the student body, and the community. His or her behavior must be compatible with the standards of right and wrong.

In dealing with students who commit a similar offense or who may be involved in the same offense, are the same disciplinary actions meted out to all the students equally, or is consideration given to how many offenses one child has had as compared to another? If corrective measures differ for the same infraction, is this policy stated in the school's discipline plan? Are students and parents aware of the school's discipline plan? As principal of a school

where many neighborhood brawls were settled at school, I had to devise a plan that would reduce the amount of time spent on dispute resolution and eliminate any doubt in the minds of parents regarding the equity of my decisions. When holding disciplinary parent conferences that involved student altercations, I scheduled everyone for the same time. Upon arrival, I would introduce the parents, explain the purpose of their presence, and identify the mediation process that would be used to obtain a fair disciplinary action. The process assured everyone that they would have an opportunity to state their case and offer a rebuttal if necessary. At the end of our conference, all parties concerned were aware of the actions that would be taken to bring closure to the incident. Did everyone get the same punishment? Sometimes yes and oftentimes no, but the parents were in support of the decisions; they understood the situation and publicly endorsed the outcomes of the conference. Some parents even apologized to the other child and family. This eliminated the question that parents often would ask, "What happened to the other child?"

There are situations that require students to receive special services or treatment because of their circumstances. If children are injured or have surgery, do you facilitate their learning by providing special accommodations at school or making arrangements for them to continue their studies while at home? With so much religious and cultural diversity in our schools, it is a necessity for school personnel to know the children that would be affected negatively with some of the usual customs and traditions followed by schools. What arrangements are made for those students when the "jolly fat man" visits the building during the month of December? When you have a child with an individual education program, is the program designed to maximize the learning as well as the success of the student? What systems are put in place to help students whose bodies are changing and open stalls in the restrooms are no longer appropriate to accommodate their needs? Have you provided for this need?

Certain staff members are very supportive of you and your ideas, do you provide them with preferential treatment over the ones who may question or take issue with you? Do you provide equal supervision to all the staff? How about all those sales people who come to your building trying to lure your business with a candy bar or a fresh bouquet of flowers, do you find yourself more inclined to be influenced by their backdoor approach to selling

something to you? Some unethical behavior is blatant, and some is very subtle. It's the subtle aspects of ethical behavior that you may not recognize in yourself, such as showing favoritism to certain staff members and students—but to others they might be easily recognizable. This can create unnecessary hostility in the work place.

A school administrator has the responsibility of working with a wide range of people: parents, teachers, students, noncertificated personnel or support staff, community leaders, and the community as a whole. He or she must have a core set of values that guide each decision that is made; this will help to avoid the convenience of questionable or rash actions and to establish the trust and respect that is needed to successfully lead others. As the principal is considered the leader of the educational unit established by the school district in neighborhoods, it is necessary that people view the leader with positive regard. As the leader is viewed, so is the school. A leader that lacks respect becomes a follower, and the organization eventually fails.

Turning Down Money From the Big Boys

Integrity of spirit is more important than any amount of money.

—Diana Williams

There was an industrial business in the neighborhood of our school. For years, the neighborhood association had been in litigation with the company over wastes and toxins that were allegedly visited upon the neighborhood, causing illness and deaths due to cancer. One of the neighborhood activists worked as a volunteer in our school. Thus, we were privy to information and updates on the litigation between the company and the neighborhood. The parents of some of the students in the school asked me if they could use the school auditorium from time to time to hold their association meetings. I agreed, as I viewed the school as a hub and extension of the neighborhood. The interaction between the neighborhood residents and the company was ongoing during my tenure in that school and had gone on for several years prior. Finally, in about the fourth year of my tenure, word went out that the community was about to win a multimillion dollar lawsuit that would give compensation to several families that had been stricken with cancer thought to be associated with the emissions from the company. Everyone was awaiting the final hearing on the matter.

During that time, a representative from the company called me to ask if there was anything they could do for my school. He in effect said that they would provide anything we wanted or needed. We were invited to give them a wish list. My instinct thought that this company was trying to buy some neighborhood good will prior to the verdict. I wondered where they had been from the beginning. I talked this development over with the staff as well and explained my thinking about it. They fully supported our commitment to the community. I said to the company representative the next time we talked, "We of course would love to have your assistance; however, since I know that you are in litigation with the families that attend this school, I respectfully request that we wait until the litigation is settled, and then we can discuss terms for your adopting our school as your project." The prospective benefactor agreed and signed off curtly. Needless to say, I never heard from them again. A few weeks later, the community prevailed in its almost-decade-old lawsuit, and the residents were awarded compensation for their losses.

My Journal Story

_____

_____

_____

_____

_____

_____

_____

_____

_____

_____

_____

_____

_____

_____

_____

_____

_____

_____

_____

_____

Lessons Learned

- Money is tempting and can entice one to lose perspective on a situation.

- Integrity of spirit is more important than any amount of money.

- It is important for the school to understand the implications of its actions on the larger community.

- It is often hard for school personnel to stand up to a larger political, financial, or social entity, yet when done, there is greater respect.

Mini Coaching

- When have you had to face an ethical dilemma?

- How did you solve the situation?

- What were the benefits and the clarity that you gained from the experience?

Just a Regular Old School

Integrity is its own reward.

—Anonymous

When I went to my new assignment from central office, several teachers greeted me warmly and expressed pleasure that I was assigned to their building. Several of them had interacted with me in my role as supervisor of professional development. But, several of them also stated sentiments like, "How long is central office going to let you stay down here with us before they pull you for another assignment?" (This had happened to my previous principal assignment six years earlier, where I had been assigned as a principal of a building for less than a year when a new superintendent pulled me for a central-office assignment that he deemed urgent.) At first, I laughed with them and said, "No way that's going to happen." But after I kept getting some variation of that same question as I interacted with my new staff, at some point I realized I would have to confront not only their perceptions, but my own apparent ambiguity about whether I would be tempted by a seductive central-office position. Despite the fact that everyone says the instructional leader is the most important job in schooling, with teaching being next, this fact is not substantiated in pay or in stature. After I thought about it, I knew what I had to do. At the next staff meeting, I addressed my future tenure in the building head on. I told them how I had enjoyed my various roles in the district, but that leading a school was the most challenging and important work, and I was committed to work with them to actualize all of the theory and programming that I believed in to make our school the best school. The caveat was that as long as we were moving and growing, I promised I would not leave to take another assignment. That pronouncement seemed to satisfy them, and from that day on, I was accepted.

The following year, another new superintendent was brokering a newly formed professional-development school. This type of school had been a dream of mine all the years I had been a staff-development administrator. He called me in to ask me if I would accept the assignment and make it a lighthouse school. I explained to him that while I would have loved the opportunity at another time, I was fully committed to working with my "regular" school to make it everything he was proposing and more for the new school. I explained how I had given my word to my staff and how hard we were working to make our school great.

I'm not sure he understood how I could pass up such a wonderful opportunity, but I left the meeting with renewed commitment for my "regular school," my promise intact and renewed clarity about the importance of integrity as a leader.

My Journal Story

_____

_____

_____

_____

_____

_____

_____

_____

_____

_____

_____

_____

_____

_____

_____

_____

_____

_____

_____

Lessons Learned

- There are politics in schooling. One can either choose to "play the game" or to be true to one's own "north compass," as described in Stephen Covey's (1990) *Principle-Centered Leadership* (p. 94).

- School leaders have to earn the trust of colleagues and then honor that trust with honesty and integrity.

- It seems that the universe will always provide challenges and tests to one's resolve. Who would have thought that a dream assignment would have come along so soon after making such a commitment and promise?

- The regular school proved to be the dream assignment as we worked to build an inspiring and effective school.

Mini Coaching

- Think of a time when your integrity has been challenged. How did you handle the dilemma?

- What was the payoff for you?

- How might the situation have turned out differently?

Cookies Are Not Everything

Only the mediocre are always at their best.

—W. Somerset Maugham, English Playwright

Bonnie Smith, one of our Title I teachers, was always welcomed into the lounge before the official school day started, but as soon as she left the room, people would laugh and talk about the weird behavior she exhibited. However, they would always acknowledge the wonderful treats that she brought to school for everyone to share. I was puzzled as to how she could act in a reclusive manner but yet bring treats for the staff, mostly the lounge crowd, to enjoy. Other teachers complained that she returned unruly students back to their classrooms without assuming any responsibility for their discipline or providing them with any instruction. The latter posed a problem that needed to be addressed. Discipline problems, even with five or six students, were inevitable due to her inability to keep the students engaged in learning activities and due to poor planning, as evidenced through observation and perusal of her lesson plans. I had several conferences with her and with the director of her program. When I discussed a special evaluation, I was actually discouraged from pursing that course of action because I was a beginning principal and my judgment would be compared to all the satisfactory evaluations from experienced principals that she had received over the course of years; she had enough years to retire.

After reflecting upon the not-so-wise advice of the program director and my own integrity, I decided that one of us would need to go; she would go because she was found not competent, or

I would go because I was incapable of evaluating teacher performance. The boxing gloves were on, and preparation for round one had begun, but a strange turn of events occurred: Our school had been identified as a visitation site by a consultant from the State Department of Education. The consultant's job was to visit each classroom and interview each staff member to determine whether our school and the district were in compliance with the State Department's mandates. The school made preparations for the visit by pulling together the required data and establishing a staff-observation schedule, which was given to everyone. For me, this visit turned out to be a miracle. Mrs. Smith refused to allow the consultant to observe her teach; when he entered her classroom she stopped all teaching activities and looked at him and the students. The consultant and I had an exit conference, and Mrs. Smith's behavior was the topic of most concern. By the end of the next day, she was removed.

The staff knew that the removal of Mrs. Smith was the best possible occurrence for our students and school. Some did lament the fact that there would be no more regular treats to eat, but the others who were directly impacted by her were relieved to know that their students would be receiving the reading assistance that they needed. For whatever reason, within a few days of her departure, she sent a floral arrangement to me.

My Journal Story

Lessons Learned

- A school district has layers of people, and each layer makes decisions based upon their knowledge, experience, or preference for dealing with difficult situations.

- School staffs are not necessarily good at policing their own unless they are directly impacted by a situation.

- In talking with some more-seasoned administrators, I learned that the problems experienced by me with this teacher were not new and that she had been moved from building to building.

- I was willing to place my career on the line if necessary in order to ensure that the needs of the school were met.

Mini Coaching

- In considering a special evaluation and possible removal of a staff member, what actions do you want to take?

- When have you confronted a difficult decision to remove a staff member in the past?

- What support and resources do you need to assist you in making your decision?

Taking the Special out of Special Education

In every story I have heard, good teachers share one trait: a strong sense of personal identity infuses their work.

—Parker Palmer, Author, Educator, and Activist

I remember the phone call as though it were this morning. My executive director was on the line and he had some exciting news to share with me: The Planning and Development Office identified an extra room in my building and they were placing a preprimary special-education unit in that room when school opened the coming school year. My heart sank because I had no recourse. I could only imagine what it would be like to have these students; I felt that having these young people would create an extra problem for me that I did not need or want. Old videotapes that depicted the students in special education being victimized on the playground by others began to play in my head, and I wanted none of that extra responsibility.

Fortunately, I had no control over the situation. The special-education unit arrived with six of the sweetest and most loveable students that you could possibly meet, along with a very capable teacher named Barbara Martin. For whatever reason, Mrs. Martin and Mrs. Barker, one of the kindergarten teachers, developed a relationship and had started to share ideas and different activities. Out of this relationship was born the idea of combining the two classes into one and having the two teachers provide services as a team. They approached me with the idea, and I listened as they explained what they wanted to do and how they were going to do it. The kindergarten room was very large, and space was not an issue. The number of students in the classroom would be approximately 30, which is a manageable number. The students in the special-education unit would be placed in a less restrictive environment, and the students in the regular class would benefit from the experience of having two teachers and learning to get along with others who might be somewhat different in their learning styles.

The two classes worked well. Unless you knew who the students in special education were, it was impossible to look at the group and make that distinction, whether in the classroom or out on the playground. The program was so successful that it inspired one of the mothers of a student in special education to join the AmeriCorps program at the Ohio State University and study to become a special-education teacher. She learned about AmeriCorps as a result of volunteering at the school and being exposed to the program as four students from the university program were assigned to our building to assist our students.

My Journal Story

_____

_____

_____

_____

_____

_____

_____

_____

_____

_____

_____

_____

_____

_____

_____

_____

_____

_____

_____

Lessons Learned

- The situation that I dreaded turned out to be one of the highlights of my career; fear most of the time resides in one's imagination.

- All of the students benefited significantly from the creativity and resourcefulness of their teachers.

- If the model is good enough, it can have a positive influence on others.

Mini Coaching

- When making organizational changes, what information would you need?

- How do you respond to staff requests for change?

- In addition to teacher enthusiasm, what else would you consider?

The PTA Caper

Ready money is Aladdin's lamp.

—Lord Byron

Cynthia Evans was the PTA treasurer, and her husband, Paul, was the president—just a really nice couple who appeared strongly committed to helping the school. As a first-year principal, I was delighted to have such support. After meeting each other and talking about how the PTA could support the work of the school, the wheels in my head started to turn, and I requested money to buy supplies for each of the classrooms. The request was granted, but we were told that we would need to wait for a couple of weeks. We waited for two weeks, then three! Finally, during the fourth week, I called to find out when we could expect the money to buy the needed classroom materials. I was assured that within the next few days the classrooms would be getting the money. When asked about the cause of the delay, I was told about the insufficient funds in the treasury and that they would need to be replenished before money could be given to the classrooms. I requested immediately that she bring the PTA's financial and business records to the school, which she did. I also informed her that one of our instructional assistants, a member of the PTA and a school parent, would be appointed as the interim treasurer until one could be officially elected. Mrs. Evans indicated that she had borrowed the money and planned to repay it, which never happened—I did not pursue the matter with the couple. Both parents were replaced as officers of the PTA.

Perhaps I dropped the ball and chose not to have the parent prosecuted, but after weighing the cost in terms of time, energy, and the recovery amount, which was difficult to determine, I decided not to expend that kind of energy. Other factors I considered included the following:

1. The amount of money that was taken—a couple of hundred dollars, as determined by the parent;

2. My lack of knowledge of the community and history of the organization outweighed the benefits and costs of filing charges against this parent;

3. The accusations would probably not be substantiated if the case were tried in court;

4. There was little chance of recovering the money; and

5. The potential value in maintaining a relationship with this parent, as she did not and would no longer have any responsibility for money.

It was more important for me to place my efforts on making sure good instruction was occurring in the classrooms. The family remained in our school and continued their involvement with our school until their children were ready to move on to middle school.

My Journal Story

_____

_____

_____

_____

_____

_____

_____

_____

_____

_____

_____

_____

_____

_____

_____

_____

_____

_____

_____

_____

Lessons Learned

- Good people are not perfect; we all have flaws.

- You have to pick your battles.

- When certain situations arise, it is necessary to take charge—we may not have been able to recover what was lost, but further abuse was eliminated.

- The relationship with the parent, a well-respected member of the school community, was salvaged, and damage to her and the school was minimized.

Mini Coaching

- In thinking about the misuse of a parent organization's funds, what actions would you take?

- What support do you need as you move forward?

- If you had a magic wand, how would this situation be resolved?

Professional-Development Snippet

Building Consensus Around Ethical Issues

Many ethical issues present themselves during the course of a school year. As they develop, collect them and provide them as scenarios for staff discussion. This could be the whole focus for one staff meeting, or you could begin each staff meeting with an ethical question.

Divide the staff into pairs by asking them to partner up with someone who is wearing the same color. In twos, discuss the assigned scenario. Allow 10 minutes to discuss. After 10 minutes, ask each pair to join another pair and come to consensus about the scenario. After 10 minutes more, have each group report out their findings about their discussion.

Scenario 1: Staff Perks

"When outside staff-development opportunities become available, only the same few staff members are selected to participate. There is never any sharing of the information obtained at these meetings."

Scenario 2: Equity in Student Assignments

"At the time of the year when student placements and grade assignments are considered for next year, teachers can be very vocal and demanding about their preferences. The principal acquiesces to the pressure of making student assignments—new and inexperience faculty members get the most difficult student assignments and the split grade, if needed. It's the way it's done here."

Scenario 3: Rock-Solid Teacher

"You have a rock-solid teacher in your building who has continually been assigned the most challenging and difficult students each year; she almost takes pride in her reputation for being the toughest teacher on staff. This year, she has requested that the wealth be shared among all the teachers at that grade level. The principal is scared 'straight' because he knows the potential for problems with a certain teacher, so he does not honor the request."

The process for football drafts has proven to be a model of building fairness into the building of football teams. The less successful teams get to choose players first. Over time, this ensures that no team is unfairly stacked with all of the best players, but each lower-performing team has a chance to build a stronger team. Should school personnel do no less than a sports team? The few scenarios cited above are just a tip of the iceberg. The school has an opportunity to explore all aspects of ethical or unethical behavior—it's a way of scrutinizing how people within the organization treat each other. Having meaningful conversation about these and other ethical issues will help your staff develop norms. Does a spirit of fairness prevail? Are rules applied evenly? Is there a prevailing spirit of high expectations? Does a culture of professionalism exist? Are tough conversations held privately? Is diversity obvious in school activities and classes? Most educational organizations as well as school districts have a code of ethics. Perhaps these professional standards could be used as a benchmark to determine how well the school is doing. The best advice I've come across is let your walk reflect the talk.

CHAPTER

Standard Six

A school administrator is an educational leader who promotes the success of all students by understanding, responding to, and influencing the larger political, social, economic, legal, and cultural context.

TUNING INTO THE LARGER CONTEXT

INTRODUCTION
Navigating the Paradoxes + Change = Resilience

When considering the phrase from Standard 6, "understanding, responding to, and influencing the larger political, social, economic, legal and cultural context," there are many opportunities that present themselves that will determine if a principal is tuning in or tuning out of the larger context. Change is the norm. Nothing stays the same for long. The world is constantly changing with regards to the political, social, economic, legal, and cultural realities of our communities. What does this fact mean for the elementary principal? The context will change depending on your own locale and constituency. As principals, we are not only called upon to understand these issues but also to respond to them. It is also not sufficient to only respond to these issues, but we are called upon to influence these factors that impact our schools. It is a paradox that while a principal can believe he is a really good principal because he holds teachers accountable, secures resources, and works hard on curriculum and instruction, he may not be regarded highly because he misses the social, political, economic, cultural, or legal nuances that make him an inspirational principal. An inspirational principal is an ambassador within the community that promotes a culture where all stakeholders want to work hard to make the school a success. Inspirational leaders instill confidence that they can respond to a wide array of issues, people, and situations that make up the larger context of our society. Inspirational leaders are adept at navigating the paradoxes of a changing world embedded in the social, economic, legal, political, and cultural issues related to schooling.

Social Context

Our schools mirror our communities. We are a part of the community. We are called upon to be visible in the community that we share. Some ways that we are called upon are

Participation in neighborhood events such as festivals and parades;

Invitations to become members of local associations;

Participation in local sporting events involving the feeder high school;

Alliances and partnerships with local businesses, churches, and social agencies; and

Visibility at significant family events, such as funerals of family members.

Economic Context

As our families suffer and survive the current economic conditions in our society, our schools will rise and fall with them. We couldn't pass our levy until we got the economically disadvantaged community involved in the passage of the levy. When traditionally the schools did not make a pitch to gain the vote of the disadvantaged, saying, "They don't care, they're apathetic," the schools were able to influence them and make them a viable part of their strategy by showing how the levy would benefit them and their children. When you influence the larger context, you reach out to all and provide the necessary outreach to the community. Other economic issues that impact our schools include

Mortgage foreclosures and job losses, which changes the school population;

Businesses failing, changing the school district tax bases;

Homelessness and the mobility of families; and

Grants and securing of additional resources to meet the needs.

Legal Context

The whole explosion in special-education law and laws to safeguard the rights of the handicapped over the decade have provided a significant paradigm shift for educators. There has always been a body of education law, but the demands on principals have become even more compelling over the last decade as we struggle to keep up with the changes. Mindful of the rights of all, safeguarding due process for all, and due diligence of all procedures are elements of being aware of the larger legal context.

Principals struggle with understanding and responding to the notion that special education means special. All students may not be treated the same but with considerations for adherence to the law. Federal laws on manifestation of disability require different behavior on the part of adults and demands adherence. Principals must influence receptivity to the law. Avoidance is no longer an option.

Other legal issues where understanding is necessary but not sufficient include

Privacy rights;

Antibullying laws;

Sexual identity and orientation issues; and

Gender issues.

Political Context

There are pulls on the schools to conform to various political entities:

The far-right, liberal pull, reacting to rules, curriculum policies, and books

Issues of global warming and groups that pressure for adherence to green policies

Global concerns and those that want to have a global orientation and those that want to be more nationalistic in scope

Activist groups for a great number of causes

Cultural Context

The cultural context includes

Religious freedoms and racial identities;

Immigration issues where we no longer deny education to undocumented children;

Homelessness issues where residency requirements do not apply;

English-as-second-language laws wherein schools are held accountable for teaching children with primary languages other than English; and

Equity issues.

Technology

One of the most dramatic shifts in context for schooling has been in the area of technology. It can be argued that technology spans all of the areas of the larger context: the economic, the legal, the cultural, and the social. But for this discussion, technology represents the greatest paradigm shift in the last decade. Consider these shifts:

Then	Now
Used cell phones for emergency only	Children and parents use as a necessity
Mainframes provided networking in schools	Mobile and Wi-Fi powering of computers
Yellow pages, maps, atlases, dictionaries	Applications
Dial-up computers	Instant browsing and connections
Phone calls, faxes, letters sent home	E-mail, texting, Facebook, Twitter communication
Checks purchase orders	Wire transactions
Report cards, grade books	Grades kept on personal data systems
Teacher observation forms	Instant-feedback technology
Chalkboards, overhead projectors	Whiteboards, SMART Boards
Newspapers, television news	Instant e-mail, pictures, and text
Encyclopedias	Wikis
Local focus	World focus
Visiting the human relations department with a resume	Being linked in

The list goes on and on. The point is that we principals have to constantly adjust to the new world that technology presents. As soon as we have mastered one piece of technological application, it is obsolete, and we must move on to the next. Thus, we must continually respond to keep our schools in the forefront of the paradigm shift.

So, we, as leaders, have to respond contextually to our work, keeping in mind the larger context of cultural, social, economic, legal, and technological. Trying to navigate all of these forces is trying and vexing. We recognize that the state of well-being of our society is contingent upon our responsiveness to everything changing. The best we can offer is to be true to ourselves and to interact with each of these entities as authentically, thoughtfully, and honestly as we can. If we can first understand our own core values then we can stay true to our own sense of integrity and commit to a level of openness and fairness. We have no way of knowing what the larger context will look like in 1, 5, or 10 years. Our role is to prepare our children for the future. We can inspire a healthy curiosity about the world we all share, a passion for working to make the world a better place, an attitude of respect for the rights and values of others as well as ourselves, and develop the mindset that we will give the best to the world.

Tradition or Trend?

Tradition simply means that we need to end what began well and continue what is worth continuing.

—Jose Bergamin, Spanish Writer

Great things are not accomplished by those who yield to trends and fads and popular opinion.

—Jack Kerouac, American Writer

During the last few decades, there has been a dramatic shift away from celebrating or recognizing certain holidays in schools and a greater emphasis on the use of the school day to focus on the students' acquisition of academic skills. The holiday that has undergone the most scrutiny in our greater educational community is Halloween. It is increasingly common to think of Halloween as having religious overtones because it has its roots in paganism and Christianity. It is largely a secular celebration, however, but some Christians and pagans have expressed strong feelings about its religious overtones. In my school community, Halloween was considered to be a time for fun and community activities, so we chose not to call our activities "harvest days" or other such referrals. The challenge for the school was to balance our day with fun and the business of learning. The first half of the day was devoted to academic activities; the presence of costumes was not permitted at any grade level. During the noon hour, the children were allowed to dress: Parents could bring costumes to school and help their children to dress; take them home; or send the costumes in a bag and members of the PTA, teachers, or other school personnel would assist if needed. Dressing and eating took about an hour. At one o'clock, we gathered in formation on the playground to start our neighborhood parade (all five hundred students). The parade went east for a couple of blocks then turned

north and passed through the cafeteria of a very large hospital—arrangements had been made to do this. We emerged out of the front entrance of the hospital, crossed the street, and whipped through the nursing home. The residents who were able handed out treats to the students as they passed by their station. It was rewarding to see the smiles on the faces of the frail and infirm; some were standing and others were sitting in wheelchairs. The parade retreated from the hospital area and continued on its journey back to school. As the parade proceeded through the neighborhood, we passed the homes of some of our students, and they proudly pointed to their houses, which did not resemble the homes pictured in *Better Homes and Gardens*; but to the children, they were their homes and you could hear the pride in their voices as they said, "that's my house." The other children were very accepting, and there was not one hint of sarcasm or negativity heard in response. Parents and others came to the corner to watch and wave. Upon our return to school, half of the student body went to the gym for the storyteller, and the other half went to their rooms for refreshments. After a half hour, the groups switched. Our day came to a close, and everyone seemed happy, including the staff. It was a good day; we were able to make others smile, hear stories from a professional storyteller, get some treats to eat, and maintain our academic focus for part of the day.

My Journal Story

_____

_____

_____

_____

_____

_____

_____

_____

_____

_____

_____

_____

_____

_____

_____

_____

Lessons Learned

- It is important to honor community traditions. It is possible to find a balance between fun and learning.

- Halloween can be a time of giving as well as receiving.

- Children view the world from their own perspective, which can be more loving, accepting, and less focused on the material aspects of the world.

Mini Coaching

- How do you align your values with community expectations?

- How do you keep the fun in schooling and maintain academic balance?

- What factors do you consider?

- What outcome would you expect from your decision and how will you know whether it was achieved?

The Tent Meeting

Wisdom is the reward you get for a lifetime of listening when you'd preferred to talk.

—Doug Larson, Newspaper Columnist and Author

One day, a gentleman came into the office and asked to speak with the principal. The secretary checked to see whether this was possible, and I was able to accommodate the request. This gentleman turned out to be an evangelist who wanted to use our school playground for a weekend revival meeting. My first inclination was to deny this request; after all, we had many storefront churches in the area, and if community people were interested in attending church, there were several other options in addition to the smaller churches. So, I skirted around the issue until he told me that he had been directed to use this school's playground by his higher power. Now, I'm not one to argue with powers such as those he alluded to, and I agreed to have the revival conducted on the grounds of the school at no facility rental charge. The meetings were held the following weekend and as luck would have it, my not-so-friendly neighbor from across the street dropped by to see what was going on; after all, he was the self-appointed "mayor" of the street. He entered the tent, stayed for the service, and was moved by some unknown power to join the church. Some of our parents also attended the services, and on Monday morning, I was informed about the sudden change in our neighbor's attitude and behavior. Evidently, this was a real transformation for him because he stopped complaining about the balls accidently flying over the fence, across the street, and occasionally onto his property; the cars parked in front of his house; my ill-mannered students; and anything else he could justify in his mind as being wrong. His whole demeanor did change for the better, and he became someone to value rather than fear.

My Journal Story

⌊L⌋

Lessons Learned

- It is wise to listen before speaking; the community's interest did not lay within the perspective of one individual, and openness to the views of others proved to be beneficial.

- When weighing the appropriateness of a situation, the answer is not always clear when there are no apparent negative consequences.

- The school facility could be a resource to the community and therefore enhance the school's image as having even greater value than just being a school.

Mini Coaching

- In thinking about community activities that involve your school or the grounds, what are the factors that influence your decisions?

- What type of guidelines would you need to establish for the use of school property by outside interests?

- What are activities that you feel would enhance your school's image and provide needed services to the community?

Cultural and Religious Differences
I Want Them to Stay in This School

As the world flattens, it is a more-realistic experience for children to naturally interact with each other than segregating them into silos of learning.

—Diana Williams

One day, a father brought his son and daughter into the school to register them. He asked to speak to the principal, and in his broken English he asked about enrolling his children. I spoke to the children and noted that they did not seem to speak English. In our district, we had an English as Second Language Welcome Center, where newly immigrated families could receive assistance and placement in one of the ESL learning centers. This program had excellent results in assimilating students into a regular school program after an orientation period. I thought they would be excellent candidates for this service. I gave the father materials and directions and told him about the program. I called the ESL center and made inquiries for him. They assured him and me that they would take care of him when he arrived. He thanked me warmly, we shook hands, and I bade the family goodbye.

The next day, bright and early, the father and his children reappeared, and the father wished to speak to me again. I asked him if I could help him and if there had been a problem. He stated emphatically that he wanted his children to stay at "this school." I assured him that I would love to have his children stay, but that I thought the ESL program would better serve the children because they spoke little English. But, he insisted, "No, this school." I told him he would not be eligible for the services to help us, but he again insisted, "No, this school." I told him I would find out what we had to do. I called the ESL department and they told me that

he had the right to refuse services and keep the children in my school. They said that they were not prepared to serve children outside of their program, but that they would help us informally.

So, I welcomed the children and placed them into classrooms. I asked him if he would mind bringing the children the next day to enable me time to plan for their arrival. He agreed, so they were enrolled. I called a meeting with the receiving teachers, third and fifth grade, later that day. We discussed ways they would incorporate the children into the classrooms. We did accept help from the ESL program. We were unsure of what lay ahead, but we jumped in and welcomed our new students.

The two children thrived in our school. They were very bright, eager, loving children and made friends easily. They picked up English quickly and became well integrated into the school routine. One day, when I saw them sitting in the office at lunchtime, Rasher told me they could not eat lunch. When I inquired why not, they responded that it was Ramadan. The staff looked up information about this holiday and made alternate arrangements for the children to visit the library during lunchtime during Ramadan. At a subsequent multicultural fair, the women of the family cooked their traditional food and brought it in.

The staff collaboration made this potentially difficult situation a successful cultural experience for all.

My Journal Story

_____

_____

_____

_____

_____

_____

_____

_____

_____

_____

_____

_____

_____

_____

_____

_____

_____

Lessons Learned

- I came to believe that it is better for ESL students to be mainstreamed into the schools. They provide a rich cultural experience for all.

- Decentralizing ESL services enables resource personnel to work in an individualized way with families.

- It takes a whole village to raise a child.

- As the world flattens, it is a more realistic experience for children to naturally interact with each other than segregating them into silos of learning.

Mini Coaching

- What are some cultural issues you are dealing with in your school?

- What have you tried that has worked?

- What resources would be most helpful in influencing the cultural context?

- What next steps could transform your cultural context?

Equity in Resources

Leveraging the Field With Grant Writing

Once you develop a template for a comprehensive grant, you understand your school processes much better.

—Diana Williams

There was a district requirement that every school would have a school-improvement plan. We dutifully wrote our plan. But, the plan became so much more than a writing exercise to satisfy a mandate. Our committees used the school-improvement plan as the basis for writing for numerous grants. There were technology grants for computers, for hiring parent volunteers, to go to the Center of Science and Industry, to take students to visit college campuses, for professional development, for safety initiatives, for science, for math experiences, and numerous other grants. (See the Chapter 4 Professional-Development Snippet: Building Parent and Community Partnerships.)

The bottom line is that we had money and resources for our children. We kept a large scrapbook documenting our grants and activities for everyone to look at when they waited in the office. (Now, we would create a CD, a Web page, or a blog to communicate our successes with our constituents.) All along the way, we informed our parent community about our grant-seeking activities to let them know that we were working on behalf of their children. Often, we invited parents in to be a part of the grants team. This is one way we were able to influence the larger economic context of a lack of resources for our school.

My Journal Story

Lessons Learned

- There are resources to help schools. It requires hard work and commitment to uncover the resources and to apply for them.

- Once you develop a template for a comprehensive grant, you understand your school processes much better. This template can be recycled for additional grants.

- It is important to get commitment from a broad base of stakeholders. It helps them to gain clarity about the school processes as well.

Mini Coaching

- What are the aspects of your school that you want to showcase?

- What resources do you need to carry out more initiatives?

- Who can you partner with to accomplish your initiative?

- How can you build consensus among your stakeholders?

The Prayer Warriors

It gave me great comfort knowing that there was a prayer community out there for my school.

—Diana Williams

At the beginning of one school year, a retired teacher whom I greatly admired came into my office and said that she was part of an initiative at a local church called "Prayer Warriors" and wanted to know if it was alright for her to come in every other week before school and pray with me for our school. I am fully aware of the separation of church and state rules, but this was one of those times when my own core values led my spirit. I agreed that before school I would appreciate a private prayer with her. So, we did that for the year. I felt I needed all the help I could get as principal.

My Journal Story

_____

_____

_____

_____

_____

_____

_____

_____

_____

_____

_____

_____

_____

_____

_____

_____

_____

_____

Lessons Learned

- I wondered about the legality of my decision, but decided that since it was on my time (before school) and a private issue with regards to my right to worship, that I was on safe ground.

- I understood that I could not proselytize the public school community.

- This was a decision I made consistent with my beliefs that gave me great comfort knowing that there was a prayer community out there for my school.

- I appreciated the thoughtfulness of the church community for public education.

Mini Coaching

- Was there ever a time when your moral compass was not aligned with the expectations of the organization?

- How did you handle it?

- What other ways might you have handled it? Think of at least five other ways!

- In what way will you prepare yourself in the event a similar situation arises?

- How do you renew your spirit?

Forget That Old Union Contract

Do not follow where the path may lead. Go instead where there is no path and leave a trail.

—Anonymous (www.leading-learning.co.nz)

After researching various school-reform programs for almost six months, the staff made a decision to model our program, with modifications, after one that had been observed by one of the site-visitation teams. The selected program had resources that we did not have, and our program or model would need to be structured around our assets. The model school had a spare classroom, personnel to implement their program, and material resources. All of our classrooms were filled with students, and there was no unassigned teacher available to coteach with the Title I teacher, and coordinating materials did not exist. Our plan called for freeing up a classroom teacher by dismantling a classroom and significantly increasing class size in the other same-grade classrooms—well beyond the limits established by the Teachers' Union. If these things could have been done without challenging the contract, there would not have been a monumental problem. Our district and the Teachers' Union had set up a system to appeal situations that might need to be amended; it was called the Variance Committee and consisted of an equal number of union and administration representatives. Most situations did not deal with the "sacred cow" of the contract, which was class size. Class size for the intermediate grades was a maximum of 30 students. Our plan would increase this number to at least 40 students or more. In order to have a contract variance considered, it must be approved by 80% of the staff. Getting the approval

of staff that was not affected would be easy. Once the realities of the situation begin to sink in, the plan started to seem less glamorous to those who would have to manage the larger number of students. The appealing part of the plan was that for part of the day, those teachers would have no more than 15 students in their rooms—the others would be in the learning lab. The learning-lab teachers were responsible for reinforcing math and reading that was taught in the classroom, rather than isolated skills. Coordination and collaboration were critical to the success of our model.

After a little lobbying and perhaps some gentle arm twisting, we were able to get the signatures needed for our variance to be considered; it was also helpful that one of the strongest proponents of the plan, a member of the site-visitation team and an intermediate teacher, would be impacted by the waiver. The waiver or variance was approved possibly because of the strong, passionate appeal by the teachers who attended the hearing. We implemented the plan the following school year. The plan was very effective; our math and reading scores improved by more than twenty points. The teachers that were impacted by the change were disgruntled at times, especially when it was time to do progress reports, but the benefits for the children far outweighed the inconveniences experienced by the staff. They, the teachers, were rewarded for their efforts.

My Journal Story

_____

_____

_____

_____

_____

_____

_____

_____

_____

_____

_____

_____

_____

_____

_____

_____

_____

_____

_____

_____

Lessons Learned

- Under certain circumstances, the most ironclad regulations can be challenged and changed.

- Involvement of the staff is critical to change; ownership revamps the individual's thinking.

- Staff members have a tremendous influence on each other, and when that energy is directed appropriately, major changes can and do occur.

Mini Coaching

- When you consider change for your school, what will it look like?

- What process will you use to create the envisioned change?

- What type of support and resources will you need?

- How will you sustain the change?

- How will you know when you are successful?

Professional-Development Snippet
Book Study

Take recommendations from staff members or other principals for book studies related to "the larger context." Once the books are identified, publish a reading list. Select one book per semester to use as a book study. Set two to three dates for the staff to come together after school to discuss the book. Divide the book into chapters, such as Chapters 1 through 4 for the first book-study session; Chapters 5 through 8 for the second session, and so on. Prepare some discussion points or questions to guide the discussion, or ask each person to develop one or two talking points or questions. Some books have accompanying workbooks or study guides. Order pizza or refreshments, and enjoy the discussion with those that attend.

Dear Principal,

I appreciate you at this school. You are no teacher, but we all know you would make a good one! You are the best principal ever!

Love,

Joey

CHAPTER

BODIES OF WORK FOR SCHOOL IMPROVEMENT

Many educators and researchers who have come before us have repeatedly reiterated the conditions that will make all students successful. We continue to be haunted by Edmonds's (1982) admonitions, "We know everything we need to know about how to improve our schools. It only remains to be seen if we are willing to do it" (p. 13). In this chapter, we have highlighted the research models that have shaped our thinking as administrators and that have enabled us to view the ISLLC standards in a comprehensive context.

The effective schools movement in the 1980s was the forerunner of much of the school-effectiveness literature that guides school improvement today. It was the antithesis to theories of schooling that blamed the circumstances in a student's life for his or her failure. The effective-schools processes analyzed factors in the educational setting that were determinants of a student's success. At a time when there were those who capitulated to the understanding that schools that served the poor could not aspire to excellence because there were too many sociological factors working against them, Edmonds (1982) was among the first to show—with research—that there were many anomalies that negated the theory that if schools were poor, they could not be instructionally effective. He developed a body of research and extrapolated correlates of effectiveness that, if evident in schools, would ensure the success of all students. This movement has shifted the burden of student success from uncontrollable variables such as poverty, race, and educational levels in the home to the sphere of influence within the school. The correlates Edmonds draws attention to are as follows.

Leadership

High expectations

Sufficient opportunity for learning

Mission

Parent and community involvement

Monitoring of student progress

Having a safe and orderly environment (pp. 13–15)

Another proponent of school reform (Comer, 1988) suggests that school reform relies on the promotion of psychological development in students, which encourages bonding to the school. The goal here was to reduce the destructive interactions among parents, teachers, and administrators and to promote structures for participation in giving cohesiveness and direction to the school's management and teaching. The governance team consisted of parents, teachers, and administrators and focused on problem solving rather than blame placing.

Barth (1990) advocated a "community of leaders" where everyone, including students, has a chance for leadership. He views the principal as the "head learner" in such a community of learners where she models and engages in the behaviors she wants teachers and students to adopt.

Anderson (1990) described the principal's role as helping to "maintain" or reproduce the institutional meanings that are incorporated in the structures, policies, and practices of the organization. Principals, furthermore, are carriers of social interchange vertically (up and down the hierarchy) and horizontally (among peers and between school and community) in space, but also across time, assuring sustainability. Other goals for leaders espoused by Anderson include helping to create an unambiguous vision and belief system; helping to seek meaning in organizational boundaries, structures, regulations, and policies; and mediating organizational paradoxes.

This translates into fostering conceptual clarity among stakeholders, commitment to excellence, and consensus building among stakeholders as the course of action for reform. This puts the principal's role front and center as the mediator of these reform efforts.

Schlechty (1990) made a case for participatory leadership as crucial to the creation of a shared vision for restructuring schools. Also, he cites evidence of restructuring efforts that have empowered and developed all employees as being the basis for recovery for certain American businesses. The assumption underlying this case is that those who are affected by decisions should be involved in them.

Levin (1988) discussed the key issues of stakeholders including (1) sharing in a unity of purpose or agreeing on a common set of goals for schooling, (2) empowerment or the ability of key participants to make important decisions at the school level and in the home to improve the education of students rather than each entity blaming the other, and (3) building on the strengths of each entity rather than exaggerating their weaknesses.

The National Association of Elementary School Administrators (NAESP, 2001) cited six characteristics of instructional leadership in its publication *Leading Learning Communities: Standards for What Elementary Principals Should Know and Be Able to Do.* The intent of these standards is to make the connection between the quality of the school, student achievement, and the principal's role, ensuring the success of all students. They cite the variables of balancing management and leadership roles, setting high expectations and standards, ensuring student achievement in agreed-upon academic standards, creating a culture of adult learning tied to student learning, using multiple data points as diagnostic tools, and actively engaging the community as attributes of leadership that principals must practice.

More recently, Alan Blankstein (2010) has written extensively about the variables that assure student success in his book *Failure Is Not an Option.* He cites the following factors as being critical for student success:

Having a common mission, vision, values, and goals;

Collaborative teaming focused on teaching for learning;

Ensuring achievement for all students by providing a system of preventions and interventions;

Using data-based decision making for continuous improvement;

Engaging the family and community; and

Building sustainable leadership capacity.

Table 7.1 organizes some of the research on effective practices in schooling.

Table 7.1   Notations of School-Improvement Bodies of Work

	Edmonds (1982)	ISLLC (1996/2007)	Blankstein (2010)	NAESP (2001)
Mission: A clearly articulated purpose for schooling	X	X	X	*Embedded
Climate: A safe, orderly environment with all personnel taking responsibility for all students	X	X	Embedded	Embedded
High expectations for all, including staff and community	X	Embedded	X—Collaborative processes	X
Sufficient opportunity for learning	X	X—Instructional program conducive to student learning and staff professional growth	X—Systems of intervention and prevention	X—Content and instruction that insures student achievement of agreed-upon academic standards
Monitoring through use of disaggregated data for baseline mastery	X	Embedded	X—Data-based	X—Use of multiple sources of data
Parent involvement	X	X—Collaborating with families and community members	X—Collaborating with families and community	X
Leadership that sets the tone for excellence	X	Embedded	X	X
Integrity, fairness, and ethics		X	Embedded	Embedded
Larger political, social, economic, legal, and cultural context		X	Embedded	Embedded
Culture of adult learning		Embedded	Embedded	X

*Note: This variable is embedded in the context of the body of work although not specifically stated as a correlate, standard, or principle. As you can see, similar themes run through all of the models.

Conclusion

It is our hope that our stories will further illuminate and personalize the educational theory that drives education today. We hope you give yourself the gift of time to reflect upon your own stories and lessons you have learned from your work. We hope that you have had a powerful experience as you tapped into your own thinking to shape the destiny of your school through your own thoughtful journaling.

We hope the mini coaching has been a mirror for your reflection. Above all, we hope for your success. Kids' lives depend on it.

We hope for schools that are nurturing and fun learning places both for adults and students, reflective of the finest aspects of our society. We hope for schools that mold the future adult citizens who will be bold avatars in a bright world.

REFERENCES

Anderson, G. L. (1990). Toward a critial constructivist approach to school to school administration. *Educational Administration Quarterly, 26*(1), 38–59.

Barth, R. (1990). A personal vision of a good school. *Phi Delta Kappan, 71*(7), 49–53.

Baughman, D. M. (1963). *Educator's handbook of stories, quotes and humor.* Englewood Cliffs, NJ: Prentice Hall.

Bernhardt, V. (2002). *The school portfolio toolkit: A planning, implementation, and evaluation guide for continuous school improvement.* Larchmont, NY: Eye on Education.

Blankstein, A. M. (2010). *Failure is not an option* (2nd ed.). Thousand Oaks, CA: Corwin.

Brooks, J. L. (Director/Writer), Zisken, L. (Producer), & Andrus, M. (Writer). (1997). *As good as it gets* [Motion picture]. United States: Tri Star Pictures.

Comer, J. P. (1988). Educating poor minority children. *Scientific American, 259*(5), 42–47.

Council of Chief State School Officers. (1996). *Interstate school leaders licensure consortium standards for school leaders.* Washington, DC: Author.

Covey, S. R. (1990). *Principle-centered leadership.* New York: Simon & Shuster.

Edmonds, R. (1982). On school improvement: A conversation with Ronal Edmonds. *Educational Leadership, 40*(3), 13–15.

Fleming, V. (Director), Leroy, M., & Freed, A. (Writers). (1939). *The Wizard of Oz* [Motion picture]. United States: Metro-Goldwyn-Mayer.

Ginott, Haim G. (1995). *Teacher and child: A book for parents and teachers.* New York: Collier.

Glasser, W. (1975). *Schools without failure.* New York: Harper & Row.

Hall, G. E., & Hord, S. M. (2006). *Implementing change: Patterns, principles, and potholes.* Boston: Allyn & Bacon.

Hall, G. E., & Loucks, S. F. (1977). A developmental model for determining whether the treatment is actually implemented. *American Educational Research Journal, 14*(3), 263–276.

Hall, G. E., & Rutherford, W. L. (1976). Concerns of teachers about implementing team teaching. *Educational Leadership, 34*(3), 227–233.

Hall, G. E., Wallace, R. C., & Dossett, W. A. (1973). *A developmental conceptualization of the adoption process within educational institutions* (Report No. 3006). Austin: The University of Texas at Austin, Research and Development Center for Teacher Education. (ERIC Document Reproduction Service No. ED095126)

Hord, S. M., Roussin, J. L., & Sommers, W. A. (2010). *Guiding professional learning communities: Inspiration, challenge, surprise, and meaning* (3rd ed.). Thousand Oaks, CA: Corwin.

Hord, S. M., & Sommers, W. A. (2008). *Leading professional learning communities: Voices from research and practice.* Thousand Oaks, CA: Corwin.

International Coach Federation. (2010). *Core competencies.* Retrieved from http://www/coachfederation.org/research-education/icf-credentials/core-competencies/

Interstate School Leaders Licensure Consortium (ISLLC). (1996/2007). *Standards for school leaders.* Washington, DC: Author.

John, E., & Rice, T. (1994). The circle of life. On *The Lion King soundtrack* [CD]. United States: Walt Disney Records.

Joyce, B., & Showers, B. (2002). *Student achievement through staff development* (3rd ed.). Alexandria, VA: Association for Supervision and Curriculum Development.

Killion, J., & Harrison, C. (2006). *Taking the lead: New roles for teachers and school-based coaches.* Oxford, OH: National Staff Development Council.

King, W. J. (n.d.). *Laura Moncur's motivational quotes.* Retrieved January 30, 2010, from http://www.quotationspage.com/quotes/King_Whitney_Jr./.

LaGravenese, R. (Writer/Director), DeVito, D., Shamberg, M., & Sher, S. (Producers). (2007). *The freedom writers* [Motion picture]. United States: Paramount Pictures.

Leslau, C. A. (1985). *African proverbs.* New York: Peter Pauper Press.

Levin, H. M. (1988). *Structuring schools for greater effectiveness with educationally disadvantaged or at-risk students.* Paper presented at the American Educational Research Association Annual Meeting, New Orleans, LA.

Lewin, K. (1951). *Field theory in social science.* New York: Harper & Row.

Lewin, K. (2006). *Resolving social conflicts: Field theory in social science.* Washington, DC: American Psychological Association.

The National Association of Elementary School Administrators. (2001). *Leading, learning communities: Standards for what elementary principals should know and be able to do.* Alexandria, VA: Author.

National Staff Development Council. (2001). *Standards for staff development* (Rev. ed.). Oxford, OH: Author.

Owings, W. A. (2003). *Best practices, best thinking, and emerging issues in school leadership.* Thousand Oaks, CA: Corwin.

Reilly, M., & Williams, D. (2008). *Leadership practices continuum.* Unpublished paper.

Schlechty, P. (1990). *Schools for the twenty-first century: Leadership imperatives for educational reform.* San Francisco: Jossey-Bass.

Steinem, G. (2009, September 28). *Leading and learning for the 21stC.* Retrieved January 30, 2010, from http://www .leading-learning.co.nz/famous-quotes.html.

Wheatley, M. J. (2002). *Turning to one another: Simple conversations to restore hope to the future.* San Francisco: Berrett Koehler.

Williams, L. (2000). *It's the little things.* Orlando, FL: Harcourt.

Wynn, M. (1993). *The eagles who thought they were chickens.* Marietta, GA: Rising Sun.

INDEX

CORWIN

A SAGE Company

The Corwin logo—a raven striding across an open book—represents the union of courage and learning. Corwin is committed to improving education for all learners by publishing books and other professional development resources for those serving the field of PreK–12 education. By providing practical, hands-on materials, Corwin continues to carry out the promise of its motto: **"Helping Educators Do Their Work Better."**